Meg's American Politics Quiz Book

2304 Questions and Answers About American Politicians

Copyright © 2019 by Meghan A. Faith

I0424679

1. Can you name the politician who received the «Heinz Award» in the year 2001?
Russell E. Train

2. Bob Graham, who belonged to the Democratic Party, became a senator in the year 1995. Which state did he represent?
Florida

3. Which award did Nicholas Murray Butler receive in the year 1931?
Nobel Peace Prize

4. Can you name the politician who received the «Wolfgang Paul Lecture» award in the year 1998?
Steven Chu

5. Chuck Robb, who belonged to the Democratic Party, became a senator in the year 1997. Which state did he represent?
Virginia

6. Can you name the politician who received the «Grand Cross 1st class of the Order of Merit of the Federal Republic of Germany» award in the year 1997?
Yehudi Menuhin

7. Name any one award Jimmy Carter received in the year 1994.
Félix Houphouët-Boigny Peace Prize

8. Name any one award Richard Lugar received in the year 2014.
Order of the Three Stars, 2nd Class

9. What medal did Eleanor Holmes Norton get in the year 1990?

Wilbur Cross Medal

10. Who wrote the book «The Peterkin Papers»?
Lucretia Peabody Hale

11. Name any one award Steve Horn received in the year 2003.
James Madison Award

12. Can you name the politician who received the «Michigan Women's Hall of Fame» award in the year 2012?
Eva McCall Hamilton

13. Bob Bennett, who belonged to the Republican Party, became a senator in the year 2009. Which state did he represent?
Utah

14. Mel Martinez became a US senator from Florida in the year 2005. Where was he born?
Sagua La Grande

15. Name any one award Paul Simon received in the year 1987.
Elijah Parish Lovejoy Award

16. In the year 1995, whom did George Pataki succeed as the Governor of New York?
Mario Cuomo

17. Jeff Bingaman became a US senator from New Mexico in the year 1997. Where was he born?
El Paso

18. In which year did Steve Bannon marry Mary Piccard?
1995

19. Where was Mike Enzi, a Republican senator from Wyoming, born?
Bremerton

20. Tom Daschle became a US senator from South Dakota in the year 2003. Where was he born?
Aberdeen

21. Marco Rubio became a senator in the year 2015. Which state did he represent?
Florida

22. Can you name the politician who received the «Nobel Prize in Physiology or Medicine» in the year 1986?
Rita Levi-Montalcini

23. Where was Jim Mountain Inhofe, a Republican senator from Oklahoma, born?
Des Moines

24. Can you name the politician who received the «Charlemagne Prize» in the year 2000?
Bill Clinton

25. Where was Peter Fitzgerald, a senator from Illinois, born?
Elgin

26. Tim Wirth became a US senator from Colorado in the year 1991. Where was he born?
Santa Fe

27. Rick Santorum became a senator in the year 1997. Which state did he represent?
Pennsylvania

28. Can you name the politician who received the «Lillian Smith Book Award» in the year 1985?
James L. Farmer, Jr.

29. Name any one award A. Philip Randolph received in the year 1989.
Labor Hall of Honor

30. Orrin Hatch became a senator in the year 1991. Which state did he represent?
Utah

31. Name any one award Ronald Reagan received in the year 2006.
California Hall of Fame

32. Patty Murray became a US senator from Washington in the year 2009. Where was she born?
Seattle

33. What is the name of Bernie Sanders's mother?
Dorothy Sanders

34. In the year 1983, whom did Toney Anaya succeed as the Governor of New Mexico?
Bruce King

35. In the year 2001, whom did Bob Wise succeed as the Governor of West Virginia?
Cecil H. Underwood

36. Can you name the politician who received the «Gandhi Peace Award» in the year 1981?
Corliss Lamont

37. In which year did Tony Earl become the Governor of Wisconsin?

38. Name any one award Franklin Delano Roosevelt received in the year 1934.
Time Person of the Year

39. Chris Dodd, who belonged to the Democratic Party, became a senator in the year 1991. Which state did he represent?
Connecticut

40. Name any one award Pierre Salinger received in the year 1981.
George Polk Award

41. Robert C. Smith became a senator in the year 1997. Which state did he represent?
New Hampshire

42. Susan Collins became a senator in the year 2007. Which state did she represent?
Maine

43. Can you name the politician who received the «David Livingstone Centenary Medal» in the year 1920?
Alexander H. Rice

44. Can you name the politician who received the «Judy Grahn Award» in the year 2015?
Barbara Smith

45. Name any one award Donald Berwick received in the year 2007.
Heinz Award

46. Where did Carina Vance Mafla get her licentiate degree in political science from?

47. Larry Craig became a senator in the year 1997. Which state did he represent?
Idaho

48. Where was Kay Hagan, a senator from North Carolina, born?
Shelby

49. Bill Nelson became a US senator from Florida in the year 2009. Where was he born?
Miami

50. Name any one award Helen Shiller received in the year 2000.
Chicago Gay and Lesbian Hall of Fame

51. Charles Ellis Schumer became a US senator from New York in the year 2015. Where was he born?
Brooklyn

52. In which year did Chet Culver become the Governor of Iowa?
2007

53. Where did Paul G. Kirk work as a chairperson in the year 1985?
Democratic National Committee

54. Charles Ellis Schumer, who belonged to the Democratic Party, became a senator in the year 2001. Which state did he represent?
New York

55. Dianne Feinstein became a US senator from California in the year 2005. Where was she born?

San Francisco

56. Tom Harkin, who belonged to the Democratic Party, became a senator in the year 2009. Which state did he represent?
Iowa

57. Name any one award Janet Yellen received in the year 2000.
honorary degree

58. Can you name the politician who received the «ASCB Public Service Award» in the year 1997?
George Gekas

59. Whom did Ben Carson marry in the year 1975?
Candy Carson

60. Larry Craig became a senator in the year 1999. Which state did he represent?
Idaho

61. What medal did John F. Kennedy receive in the year 1945?
Asiatic-Pacific Campaign Medal

62. From which university did Lucy McBath get her bachelor's degree in political science?
Virginia State University

63. Steve Daines, who belonged to the Republican Party, became a senator in the year 2015. Which state did he represent?
Montana

64. In which year did Judd Gregg become the Governor of New Hampshire?

65. Mike Johanns became a senator in the year 2009. Which state did he represent?
Nebraska

66. Can you name the politician who received the «Horatio Alger Award» in the year 1983?
Gerald Ford

67. Max Baucus became a US senator from Montana in the year 1991. Where was he born?
Helena

68. Can you name the politician who received the «Sagamore of the Wabash» award in the year 2003?
John R. Gregg

69. Name any one award Hillary Clinton received in the year 1994.
Gallup's most admired man and woman poll

70. Who wrote the book «The Rise and Fall of the Confederate Government»?
Jefferson Davis

71. Whom did Marco Rubio marry in the year 1998?
Jeanette Dousdebes Rubio

72. Where did Janet Yellen work as an academic lecturer in the year 1978?
London School of Economics

73. Where was Jim Sasser, a senator from Tennessee, born?
Memphis

74. Name any one award Jacqueline Cochran received in the year 1971.
National Aviation Hall of Fame

75. Where did Eugene Louis Dodaro get his Bachelor of Arts degree in accounting from?
Lycoming College

76. Where did Josh Harder get his bachelor's degree in economics from?
Stanford University

77. Who had hired William J. Jefferson as a law clerk in the year 1972?
Alvin Benjamin Rubin

78. Can you name the politician who received the «John Fritz Medal» in the year 1929?
Herbert Hoover

79. Phil Gramm, who belonged to the Republican Party, became a senator in the year 1993. Which state did he represent?
Texas

80. From which university did Peter Plympton Smith get his Bachelor of Arts degree in history?
Princeton University

81. Don Nickles became a US senator from Oklahoma in the year 1991. Where was he born?
Ponca City

82. What is the name of Al Gore's mother?
Pauline LaFon Gore

83. Can you name the politician who received the

«Colorado Women's Hall of Fame» award in the year 1991?
Wilma Webb

84. Where was Mary Kathryn Heitkamp, a Democratic senator from North Dakota, born?
Breckenridge

85. Can you name the politician who received the «Moskowitz Prize for Zionism» in the year 2015?
Yehuda Glick

86. Where was Donald W. Riegle, Jr., a Democratic senator from Michigan, born?
Flint

87. From which university did Joe Walsh get his Bachelor of Arts degree in English?
University of Iowa

88. Whom did Bob Ehrlich marry in the year 1993?
Kendel Ehrlich

89. George Voinovich became a US senator from Ohio in the year 2009. Where was he born?
Cleveland

90. Can you name the politician who received the «Labor Hall of Honor» award in the year 1995?
Arthur Goldberg

91. Whom did John Kerry marry in the year 1970?
Julia Thorne

92. Whom did Kellyanne Conway marry in the year 2001?
George T. Conway III

93. Mark Begich, who belonged to the Democratic Party, became a senator in the year 2013. Which state did he represent?
Alaska

94. Who had hired Mike Crapo as a law clerk in the year 1977?
James Marshall Carter

95. Name any one award William Bauchop Wilson received in the year 2007.
Labor Hall of Honor

96. In the year 1977, Marcy Kaptur worked as an assistant director in which government agency?
Executive Office of the President of the United States

97. Name any one award Mike Delph received in the year 2005.
Sagamore of the Wabash

98. In which year did Jim Edgar become the Governor of Illinois?
1991

99. Where was Paul Sarbanes, a Democratic senator from Maryland, born?
Salisbury

100. Who wrote the book «Crippled America»?
Donald Trump

101. Deb Fischer worked as a member of which high school in the year 1990?
Valentine High School

102. Herb Kohl became a senator in the year 1991. Which

state did he represent?
Wisconsin

103. Lamar Alexander, who belonged to the Republican Party, became a senator in the year 2003. Which state did he represent?
Tennessee

104. Can you name the politician who received the «Chicago Gay and Lesbian Hall of Fame» award in the year 1997?
Mary Ann Smith

105. In the year 2003, whom did Craig Benson succeed as the Governor of New Hampshire?
Jeanne Shaheen

106. Name any one award John Glenn received in the year 2008.
Theodore Roosevelt Award

107. Jon Kyl became a US senator from Arizona in the year 2005. Where was he born?
Oakland

108. Russ Feingold, who belonged to the Democratic Party, became a senator in the year 2009. Which state did he represent?
Wisconsin

109. Can you name the politician who received the «Golden Horse Award for Best Leading Actor» in the year 1983?
Jackie Chan

110. Thad Cochran became a senator in the year 2003. Which state did he represent?

Mississippi

111. From which university did Aftab Pureval get his Bachelor of Arts degree in political science?
Ohio State University

112. In the year 1977, whom did Jim Hunt succeed as the Governor of North Carolina?
James Holshouser

113. In which year did Kathleen Blanco become the Governor of Louisiana?
2004

114. In the year 1990, J. C. Watts was a member of which government agency?
Oklahoma Corporation Commission

115. Ed Markey became a senator in the year 2017. Which state did he represent?
Massachusetts

116. Can you name the politician who received the «Theodore Roosevelt Award» in the year 1993?
Lamar Alexander

117. Name any one award Steven Chu received in the year 1994.
Williams F. Meggers Award

118. Where was Gordon H. Smith, a senator from Oregon, born?
Pendleton

119. Who replaced Frank Murkowski as the senator from Alaska in the year 1981?
Lisa Murkowski

120. What medal did Barack Obama get in the year 2013?
Presidential Medal of Distinction

121. Name any one award Winona LaDuke received in the year 1996.
Thomas Merton Award

122. Who wrote the book «Woodstock Nation»?
Abbie Hoffman

123. Harry Reid became a US senator from Nevada in the year 2005. Where was he born?
Searchlight

124. Can you name the politician who received the «Women's Caucus for Art Lifetime Achievement Award» in the year 1980?
Bella Abzug

125. Can you name the politician who received the «Light of Truth Award» in the year 2009?
Julia V. Taft

126. Whom did Wayne Allard replace as the senator from Colorado in the year 1997?
Hank Brown

127. David Vitter became a US senator from Louisiana in the year 2007. Where was he born?
New Orleans

128. Can you name the politician who received the «Theodor Heuss award» in the year 2006?
James Wolfensohn

129. Where was Jim Talent, a Republican senator from

Missouri, born?
Des Peres

130. Joni Ernst became a US senator from Iowa in the year 2017. Where was she born?
Red Oak

131. What is the name of Susan Collins's mother?
Patricia M. Collins

132. Can you name the politician who received the «Spingarn Medal» in the year 2003?
Constance Baker Motley

133. Carol Moseley Braun became a US senator from Illinois in the year 1993. Where was she born?
Chicago

134. Can you name the politician who received the «Wilbur Cross Medal» in the year 1997?
Janet Yellen

135. In which year did Tulsi Gabbard marry Eduardo Tamayo?
2002

136. In the year 1977, whom did James R. Thompson succeed as the Governor of Illinois?
Dan Walker

137. Whom did Donald Trump marry in the year 2005?
Melania Trump

138. Can you name the politician who received the «Washington Award» in the year 1944?
Henry Ford

139. Where was John Barrasso, a Republican senator from Wyoming, born?
Reading

140. In which year did Jennifer Granholm become the Governor of Michigan?
2003

141. John Boozman, who belonged to the Republican Party, became a senator in the year 2013. Which state did he represent?
Arkansas

142. Blanche Lincoln became a senator in the year 2001. Which state did she represent?
Arkansas

143. In which year did George Allen become the Governor of Virginia?
1994

144. Whom did Jake Garn replace as the senator from Utah in the year 1974?
Wallace F. Bennett

145. Can you name the politician who received the «Grand Cordon of the order of Nichan Iftikhar» award in the year 1943?
Dwight D. Eisenhower

146. Can you name the politician who received the «Albert Lasker Award for Basic Medical Research» in the year 1986?
Rita Levi-Montalcini

147. Name any one award Thomas J. Mabry received in the year 1954.

148. Can you name the politician who received the «Order of the German Eagle» award in the year 1938?
Henry Ford

149. Can you name the politician who received the «Officer of the National Order of Quebec» award in the year 2010?
James H. Douglas, Jr.

150. Can you name the politician who received the «Labor Hall of Honor» award in the year 1989?
Frances Perkins

151. Can you name the politician who received the «Time Person of the Year» award in the year 1972?
Richard Nixon

152. In which year did John H. Sununu become the Governor of New Hampshire?
1983

153. Can you name the politician who received the «Enrico Fermi Award» in the year 1992?
Harold Brown

154. From which university did Michael Bloomberg get his Bachelor of Science degree in electrical engineering?
Johns Hopkins University

155. Who became the mayor of Waterville in the year 2012?
Karen Heck

156. Patty Murray became a US senator from Washington in the year 1993. Where was she born?

Seattle

157. Can you name the politician who received the «Charles Frankel Prize» in the year 1994?
Sharon Percy Rockefeller

158. Name any one award Charles Erwin Wilson received in the year 1955.
Washington Award

159. In the year 1991, whom did Brereton Jones succeed as the Governor of Kentucky?
Wallace G. Wilkinson

160. Name any one award Hillary Clinton received in the year 2005.
National Women's Hall of Fame

161. From which university did John Grisham get his Bachelor of Science degree in accounting?
Mississippi State University

162. Name any one award William Porter Payne received in the year 1997.
Theodore Roosevelt Award

163. Jon Tester became a senator in the year 2007. Which state did he represent?
Montana

164. Can you name the politician who received the «California Hall of Fame» award in the year 2010?
Pat Brown

165. Can you name the politician who received the «Michigan Women's Hall of Fame» award in the year 1983?

Josephine Gomon

166. Scott Brown became a US senator from Massachusetts in the year 2010. Where was he born?
Kittery

167. Who had hired Ed Pastor as an employee in the year 1971?
Raúl Héctor Castro

168. Can you name the politician who received the «Harold W. McGraw Prize in Education» in the year 2000?
Rod Paige

169. Max Baucus became a senator in the year 1999. Which state did he represent?
Montana

170. Where was Kay Bailey Hutchison, a Republican senator from Texas, born?
Galveston

171. Name any one award Madeleine Albright received in the year 2001.
Elizabeth Blackwell Award

172. What medal did William Anderson receive in the year 1959?
Founder's Medal

173. In the year 2000, whom did Roger B. Wilson succeed as the Governor of Missouri?
Mel Carnahan

174. Can you name the politician who received the «James Madison Award» in the year 1991?
Don Edwards

175. Where was Sherrod Brown, a Democratic senator from Ohio, born?
Mansfield

176. Byron Dorgan became a senator in the year 1995. Which state did he represent?
North Dakota

177. Name any one award Charles G. Dawes received in the year 1925.
Nobel Peace Prize

178. Can you name the politician who received the «Freedom Award» in the year 1981?
Lane Kirkland

179. Where was Marco Rubio, a Republican senator from Florida, born?
Miami

180. What is the name of Marco Rubio's mother?
Oriales Rubio

181. Whom did Gary Johnson marry in the year 1977?
Dee Johnson

182. Can you name the politician who received the «Francis Parkman Prize» in the year 1957?
George F. Kennan

183. Name any one award Byron White received in the year 1969.
Theodore Roosevelt Award

184. Where was Tom Udall, a Democratic senator from New Mexico, born?

Tucson

185. In the year 1979, whom did Bob Graham succeed as the Governor of Florida?
Reubin Askew

186. Name any one award James Wolfensohn received in the year 2011.
honorary doctor of the Hebrew University of Jerusalem

187. Where did Kenneth A. Gibson get his Bachelor of Science degree in civil engineering from?
Newark College of Engineering

188. Roland Burris became a senator in the year 2009. Which state did he represent?
Illinois

189. Where was Dianne Feinstein, a Democratic senator from California, born?
San Francisco

190. Who became the mayor of Naperville in the year 1995?
A. George Pradel

191. What medal did Edward L. Ayers receive in the year 2003?
Wilbur Cross Medal

192. Who replaced Tom Harkin as the senator from Iowa in the year 1985?
Joni Ernst

193. Where did Melvin Carter III get his master's degree in public policy from?
Hubert H. Humphrey School of Public Affairs

194. In which year did Terry McAuliffe become the Governor of Virginia?
2014

195. What is the name of Jared Polis's mother?
Susan Polis Schutz

196. What medal did John Conyers get in the year 2007?
Spingarn Medal

197. In which year did Christine Gregoire become the Governor of Washington?
2005

198. Name any one award Lawrence Summers received in the year 1987.
Fellow of the American Academy of Arts and Sciences

199. Can you name the politician who received the «Nobel Peace Prize» in the year 1919?
Woodrow Wilson

200. Jim DeMint became a US senator from South Carolina in the year 2005. Where was he born?
Greenville

201. Can you name the politician who received the «Bronze Star Medal» in the year 2004?
Seth Moulton

202. What is the name of Gwen Graham's mother?
Adele Khoury Graham

203. Roger Wicker became a US senator from Mississippi in the year 2017. Where was he born?
Pontotoc

204. In the year 1995, whom did Carl T.C. Gutierrez succeed as the Governor of Guam?
Joseph Franklin Ada

205. Who replaced Chris Dodd as the senator from Connecticut in the year 1981?
Richard Blumenthal

206. Can you name the politician who received the «Honorary doctor at the Nanjing University» award in the year 1998?
George H. W. Bush

207. What is the name of Michelle Obama's father?
Fraser C. Robinson III

208. In the year 2003, whom did Mitt Romney succeed as the Governor of Massachusetts?
Jane Swift

209. In the year 1979, whom did Dick Thornburgh succeed as the Governor of Pennsylvania?
Milton Shapp

210. Whom did Rudy Giuliani marry in the year 1984?
Donna Hanover

211. Name any one award Charles A. Sprague received in the year 1955.
Elijah Parish Lovejoy Award

212. Mike Crapo became a senator in the year 2017. Which state did he represent?
Idaho

213. Can you name the politician who received the «ASCB

Public Service Award» in the year 1995?
John Porter

214. Name any one award Katie G. Dorsett received in the year 2010.
North Carolina Women's Hall of Fame

215. Can you name the politician who received the «Lasker-Bloomberg Public Service Award» in the year 1995?
Mark Hatfield

216. Ron Lee Wyden became a US senator from Oregon in the year 2013. Where was he born?
Wichita

217. Name any one award Ronald Reagan received in the year 1960.
star on Hollywood Walk of Fame

218. Whom did Nancy Pelosi marry in the year 1963?
Paul Pelosi

219. Joe Donnelly, who belonged to the Democratic Party, became a senator in the year 2017. Which state did he represent?
Indiana

220. David Pryor became a US senator from Arkansas in the year 1991. Where was he born?
Camden

221. Can you name the politician who received the «Knight Grand Cross of the Order of Merit of the Italian Republic» award in the year 1988?
Richard Nixon

222. Name any one award Margaret Chase Smith received in the year 1991.
Elizabeth Blackwell Award

223. Thad Cochran became a US senator from Mississippi in the year 1991. Where was he born?
Pontotoc

224. Who replaced Sam Brownback as the senator from Kansas in the year 1996?
Jerry Moran

225. Lindsey Graham became a US senator from South Carolina in the year 2009. Where was he born?
Central

226. In which year did Kathleen Sebelius become the Governor of Kansas?
2003

227. Name any one award Lawrence Lau received in the year 2012.
honorary doctor of the Fudan University

228. Where was David Durenberger, a senator from Minnesota, born?
St. Cloud

229. Can you name the politician who received the «James Madison Award» in the year 2001?
John Podesta

230. Where did Brett Kavanaugh get his Bachelor of Arts degree in history from?
Yale College

231. Name any one award Benjamin Spock received in the

year 1968.
Gandhi Peace Award

232. Where did Charlene Drew Jarvis get her Doctor of Philosophy degree in neuropsychology from?
University of Maryland

233. Can you name the politician who received the «Adam Smith Award» in the year 2010?
Janet Yellen

234. Name any one award Ron Dellums received in the year 2000.
Thomas Merton Award

235. Lindsey Graham became a US senator from South Carolina in the year 2015. Where was he born?
Central

236. What medal did J. William Fulbright get in the year 1977?
Benjamin Franklin Medal

237. In the year 2009, whom did Bev Perdue succeed as the Governor of North Carolina?
Mike Easley

238. Can you name the politician who received the «Knight Commander's Cross of the Order of Merit of the Federal Republic of Germany» award in the year 2012?
David Petraeus

239. Can you name the politician who received the «National Women's Hall of Fame» award in the year 1982?
Carrie Chapman Catt

240. Whom did Bob Wise marry in the year 1984?

241. Can you name the politician who received the «August Wilhelm von Hofmann Medal» in the year 1939?
Albert Szent-Györgyi

242. Where did Edwin Erickson get his Bachelor of Science degree in biology from?
Albright College

243. Can you name the politician who received the «H. H. Bloomer Award» in the year 1998?
William C. Wright

244. Can you name the politician who received the «Ralph W. Gerard Prize» in the year 1985?
Rita Levi-Montalcini

245. Where was Ron Lee Wyden, a Democratic senator from Oregon, born?
Wichita

246. Can you name the politician who received the «Adam Smith Award» in the year 2009?
Lawrence Summers

247. Where was John Ashcroft, a Republican senator from Missouri, born?
Chicago

248. Can you name the politician who received the «Commander's Cross of the Order of Merit of the Federal Republic of Germany» award in the year 2015?
Ronald Lauder

249. Can you name the politician who received the «Freedom Award» in the year 1999?

250. Who replaced John Ashcroft as the senator from Missouri in the year 1995?
Jean Carnahan

251. Can you name the politician who received the «honorary doctor of Harvard University» award in the year 2014?
George H. W. Bush

252. Whom did John E. Sununu replace as the senator from New Hampshire in the year 2003?
Robert C. Smith

253. Whom did John McCain marry in the year 1965?
Carol McCain

254. Claire McCaskill became a US senator from Missouri in the year 2013. Where was she born?
Rolla

255. What is the name of Ted Kennedy's father?
Joseph P. Kennedy, Sr.

256. John Hoeven, who belonged to the Republican Party, became a senator in the year 2013. Which state did he represent?
North Dakota

257. In the year 1970, Donald M. Payne was the president of which international organization?
YMCA

258. From which university did Sammuel Sanes get his associate degree in Legal management?
Keiser University

259. Whom did Mo Cowan replace as the senator from Massachusetts in the year 2013?
John Kerry

260. In the year 1987, whom did John R. McKernan succeed as the Governor of Maine?
Joseph E. Brennan

261. What is the name of Barack Obama's mother?
Ann Dunham

262. In the year 1995, whom did Jim Geringer succeed as the Governor of Wyoming?
Mike Sullivan

263. Whom did Lisa Murkowski marry in the year 1987?
Verne Martell

264. Deb Fischer became a senator in the year 2013. Which state did she represent?
Nebraska

265. Name any one award Al Gore received in the year 2007.
Nobel Peace Prize

266. In which year did Eric Greitens become the Governor of Missouri?
2017

267. In the year 1981, Joe Wilson worked as a general counsel in which energy ministry?
United States Department of Energy

268. Who replaced Richard Lugar as the senator from Indiana in the year 1977?

Joe Donnelly

269. In the year 1997, Janet Yellen worked as a chairperson in which government agency?
Council of Economic Advisers

270. Name any one award Lawrence Lessig received in the year 2014.
Webby Lifetime Achievement Award

271. Name any one award George H. W. Bush received in the year 1986.
Theodore Roosevelt Award

272. Can you name the politician who received the «Princess of Asturias Award for International Cooperation» in the year 2007?
Al Gore

273. Whom did Kelly Knight Craft marry in the year 2016?
Joe Craft

274. What medal did Peter Norbeck receive in the year 1932?
Pugsley Medal

275. Can you name the politician who received the «National Medal of Arts» in the year 2009?
Joseph P. Riley, Jr.

276. Can you name the politician who received the «Sarnat Prize» in the year 2000?
Rosalynn Carter

277. In which year did Sharon Pratt Kelly marry Arrington Dixon?
1967

278. Can you name the politician who received the «doctor honoris causa» award in the year 2008?
Rita Levi-Montalcini

279. Whom did Gaston Caperton marry in the year 1990?
Rachael Worby

280. Mark Warner became a US senator from Virginia in the year 2017. Where was he born?
Indianapolis

281. Where did Charlene Drew Jarvis get her Bachelor of Science degree in psychology from?
Oberlin College

282. Whom did Bob Bennett replace as the senator from Utah in the year 1993?
Jake Garn

283. In which year did Jeb Bush marry Columba Bush?
1974

284. Where did Jerry Moran work as a vice president in the year 1993?
University of Kansas School of Law

285. From which university did Karen Heck get her master's degree in human development?
University of Maine

286. What is the name of Donald Trump's father?
Fred Trump

287. Who had hired Don Bacon as a member of congressional staff in the year 2014?
Jeff Fortenberry

288. Can you name the politician who received the «honorary doctor of the Shanghai Jiao Tong University» award in the year 2010?
Elaine Chao

289. Can you name the politician who received the «Audubon Medal» in the year 1985?
Cecil D. Andrus

290. Jim Talent became a US senator from Missouri in the year 2002. Where was he born?
Des Peres

291. Can you name the politician who received the «Lasker-Bloomberg Public Service Award» in the year 1993?
Paul Rogers

292. Name any one award Dawn Clark Netsch received in the year 1995.
Chicago Gay and Lesbian Hall of Fame

293. In which year did Mike Leavitt become the Governor of Utah?
1993

294. Kelly Ayotte became a US senator from New Hampshire in the year 2015. Where was she born?
Nashua

295. Name any one award Steven Chu received in the year 2008.
honorary doctor of the Peking University

296. Name any one award Roald Sagdeev received in the year 2001.

James Clerk Maxwell Prize in Plasma Physics

297. Richard Bryan became a US senator from Nevada in the year 1991. Where was he born?
Washington, D.C.

298. Name any one award Rachel B. Noel received in the year 1996.
Colorado Women's Hall of Fame

299. Who became the mayor of Seattle in the year 2010?
Michael McGinn

300. What medal did Philip Lader receive in the year 2001?
Benjamin Franklin Medal

301. Johnny Isakson became a senator in the year 2017. Which state did he represent?
Georgia

302. Name any one award John McCain received in the year 2001.
Freedom Award

303. What is the name of Ivanka Trump's father?
Donald Trump

304. Name any one award Richard Armitage received in the year 2010.
Companion of the Order of Australia

305. Can you name the politician who received the «Nansen Refugee Award» in the year 1954?
Eleanor Roosevelt

306. Can you name the politician who received the

«Presidential Medal of Freedom» in the year 1963?
John F. Kennedy

307. Can you name the politician who received the «Grand Cross of the Order of Merit of Hungary» award in the year 2011?
János Horváth

308. Can you name the politician who received the «Brahms-Preis» award in the year 1990?
Yehudi Menuhin

309. Can you name the politician who received the «Chicago Gay and Lesbian Hall of Fame» award in the year 2007?
Carol Moseley Braun

310. Name any one award A. Philip Randolph received in the year 1970.
Humanist of the Year

311. Name any one award Tom Harkin received in the year 1994.
ASCB Public Service Award

312. Harry Reid, who belonged to the Democratic Party, became a senator in the year 2013. Which state did he represent?
Nevada

313. What is the name of Alison Lundergan Grimes's mother?
Charlotte Lundergan

314. Kit Bond became a senator in the year 2005. Which state did he represent?
Missouri

315. Name any one award Jacqueline Cochran received in the year 1938.
Bendix Trophy

316. In the year 1968, Jim Jeffords worked as a delegate in which political party?
Vermont Republican Party

317. Can you name the politician who received the «United Nations Prize in the Field of Human Rights» in the year 1968?
Eleanor Roosevelt

318. Can you name the politician who received the «Purple Heart» award in the year 1945?
John F. Kennedy

319. Can you name the politician who received the «Elizabeth Blackwell Award» in the year 1985?
Sandra Day O'Connor

320. Where did Alexander Acosta get his Bachelor of Arts degree in economics from?
Harvard College

321. In which year did Alison Lundergan Grimes marry Andrew Grimes?
2006

322. Where was Byron Dorgan, a Democratic senator from North Dakota, born?
Dickinson

323. Who became the mayor of Manchester in the year 2000?
Robert A. Baines

324. Who became the mayor of Frederick in the year 1974?
Ronald N. Young

325. In the year 1987, whom did Carroll A. Campbell, Jr. succeed as the Governor of South Carolina?
Richard Riley

326. Name any one award Hillary Clinton received in the year 1995.
doctor honoris causa

327. Lincoln Chafee became a US senator from Rhode Island in the year 2005. Where was he born?
Warwick

328. In which year did Pierre Samuel du Pont IV become the Governor of Delaware?
1977

329. What is the name of Boris Johnson's father?
Stanley Johnson

330. Name any one award John Lewis received in the year 1999.
Anisfield-Wolf Book Awards

331. Where did David L. Bernhardt get his Bachelor of Arts degree in political science from?
University of Northern Colorado

332. What is the name of Caroline Kennedy's mother?
Jacqueline Kennedy Onassis

333. Whom did Judd Gregg replace as the senator from New Hampshire in the year 1993?

334. Can you name the politician who received the «Rachel Carson Award» in the year 2005?
Bernadette Castro

335. Zell Miller became a senator in the year 2001. Which state did he represent?
Georgia

336. Patty Murray became a US senator from Washington in the year 2017. Where was she born?
Seattle

337. Where was Mike Lee, a Republican senator from Utah, born?
Mesa

338. Name any one award Winona LaDuke received in the year 2007.
National Women's Hall of Fame

339. In which year did Elaine Chao marry Mitch McConnell?
1993

340. Name any one award Mifflin Wistar Gibbs received in the year 2017.
Arkansas Black Hall of Fame

341. In which year did John Hoeven become the Governor of North Dakota?
2000

342. Name any one award Hillary Clinton received in the year 1997.
Gallup's most admired man and woman poll

343. Can you name the politician who received the «Fellow of the Association for Computing Machinery» award in the year 1994?
Herbert A. Simon

344. Name any one award Upton Sinclair received in the year 1943.
Pulitzer Prize for Fiction

345. In which year did Ed Rendell become the Governor of Pennsylvania?
2003

346. John Hoeven, who belonged to the Republican Party, became a senator in the year 2017. Which state did he represent?
North Dakota

347. Name any one award Michael Bloomberg received in the year 2009.
Lasker-Bloomberg Public Service Award

348. Name any one award Hillary Clinton received in the year 2009.
Margaret Sanger Awards

349. Who had hired Jay Carney as White House Press Secretary in the year 2011?
Barack Obama

350. In the year 1981, Nancy Pelosi worked as the party chair in which political party?
California Democratic Party

351. Can you name the politician who received the «Presidential Medal of Freedom» in the year 2009?

Harvey Milk

352. Can you name the politician who received the «Presidential Medal of Freedom» in the year 2004?
Edward Brooke

353. Can you name the politician who received the «Theatre World Award» in the year 1946?
Wendell Corey

354. In the year 1986, Hillary Clinton worked as a chairperson in which nonprofit organization?
Children's Defense Fund

355. In which year did Evan Bayh become the Governor of Indiana?
1989

356. What medal did Richard Lugar get in the year 2007?
Four Freedoms Award - Freedom Medal

357. Who became the mayor of Port Orange in the year 2000?
Dorothy Hukill

358. Can you name the politician who received the «Henry Laurence Gantt Medal» in the year 1968?
J. Erik Jonsson

359. Name any one award Mel Sembler received in the year 2000.
Honorary Officer of the Order of Australia

360. Who had hired James A. Barcia as an administrative assistant in the year 1975?
Donald J. Albosta

361. Can you name the politician who received the «Presidential Medal of Freedom» in the year 1998?
Dante Fascell

362. In which year did Dexter Lehtinen marry Ileana Ros-Lehtinen?
1984

363. In which year did Nikki Haley become the Governor of South Carolina?
2011

364. In the year 2002, whom did Mark Warner succeed as the Governor of Virginia?
Jim Gilmore

365. Who had hired Barbara Comstock as a member of congressional staff in the year 1991?
Frank Wolf

366. From which university did Lisa Murkowski get her Bachelor of Arts degree in economics?
Georgetown University

367. Bob Packwood became a US senator from Oregon in the year 1991. Where was he born?
Portland

368. What is the name of Martin O'Malley's mother?
Barbara O'Malley

369. Dianne Feinstein became a US senator from California in the year 1997. Where was she born?
San Francisco

370. Who had hired Ron Barber as an employee in the year 2007?

Gabrielle Giffords

371. In which year did Roy Schneider become the Governor of the United States Virgin Islands?
1995

372. Name any one award Rebecca Blank received in the year 2015.
Daniel Patrick Moynihan Prize

373. Can you name the politician who received the «Abbot Payson Usher Prize» in the year 1961?
Robert Woodbury

374. Where was Blanche Lincoln, a senator from Arkansas, born?
Helena

375. Can you name the politician who received the «Peace Prize of Hesse» in the year 1999?
George John Mitchell Jr.

376. Name any one award J. Raymond Jones received in the year 1990.
American Book Awards

377. Whom did Ray Hutchison marry in the year 1978?
Kay Bailey Hutchison

378. Can you name the politician who received the «Theodore Roosevelt Award» in the year 1973?
Omar Bradley

379. Can you name the politician who received the «William Procter Prize for Scientific Achievement» in the year 1980?
Herbert A. Simon

380. Name any one award Elizabeth Warren received in the year 2011.
Oklahoma Hall of Fame

381. Where was Don Nickles, a Republican senator from Oklahoma, born?
Ponca City

382. Where was Robert Menendez, a Democratic senator from New Jersey, born?
Uranus

383. Can you name the politician who received the «Philippine Legion of Honor» award in the year 2013?
Hillary Clinton

384. Can you name the politician who received the «Michigan Women's Hall of Fame» award in the year 1995?
Laura Freele Osborn

385. What is the name of Beto O'Rourke's father?
Pat O'Rourke

386. Name any one award Leverett Saltonstall received in the year 1968.
Theodore Roosevelt Award

387. What is the name of Lawrence Summers's mother?
Anita Summers

388. Barbara Mikulski became a senator in the year 2003. Which state did she represent?
Maryland

389. What is the name of John V. Tunney's father?

Gene Tunney

390. Russ Feingold became a senator in the year 1993. Which state did he represent?
Wisconsin

391. Whom did Scott Walker marry in the year 1993?
Tonette Walker

392. Can you name the politician who received the «Anisfield-Wolf Book Awards» in the year 1966?
Malcolm X

393. John F. Reed became a US senator from Rhode Island in the year 2003. Where was he born?
Providence

394. In the year 2006, whom did Sarah Palin succeed as the Governor of Alaska?
Frank Murkowski

395. Can you name the politician who received the «honorary doctor of the University of Gothenburg» award in the year 2007?
Hillary Clinton

396. In which year did Mitch McConnell marry Sherrill Redmon?
1968

397. Can you name the politician who received the «TED Prize» in the year 2007?
Bill Clinton

398. Can you name the politician who received the «Grand Officer of the Order of Merit of the Italian Republic» award in the year 1957?

399. Chuck Robb became a US senator from Virginia in the year 1999. Where was he born?
Phoenix

400. Susan Collins became a US senator from Maine in the year 1997. Where was she born?
Caribou

401. Bob Bennett became a US senator from Utah in the year 1997. Where was he born?
Salt Lake City

402. Joe Lieberman became a US senator from Connecticut in the year 2005. Where was he born?
Stamford

403. From which university did Thelma Buchholdt get her Bachelor of Arts degree in zoology?
Mount Saint Mary's University in Los Angeles

404. Whom did Al Gore marry in the year 1970?
Tipper Gore

405. Tom Harkin became a senator in the year 1991. Which state did he represent?
Iowa

406. Can you name the politician who received the «NAACP Image Award – President's Award» in the year 2001?
Bill Clinton

407. Who became the mayor of Athens in the year 1992?
Dan Williams

408. Whom did John Hickenlooper marry in the year 2002?
Helen Thorpe

409. In which year did Marjorie Margolies-Mezvinsky marry Edward Mezvinsky?
1975

410. Who had hired Doris Matsui as an employee in the year 1992?
Bill Clinton

411. Whom did Susan Molinari marry in the year 1994?
Bill Paxon

412. In which year did Don Sundquist become the Governor of Tennessee?
1995

413. In the year 1999, whom did Bob Taft succeed as the Governor of Ohio?
Nancy Hollister

414. Who replaced Conrad Burns as the senator from Montana in the year 1989?
Jon Tester

415. Where was Rick Santorum, a Republican senator from Pennsylvania, born?
Winchester

416. What medal did Richard Lugar get in the year 2001?
Democracy Service Medal

417. Name any one award John P. Saylor received in the year 1971.
Sierra Club John Muir Award

418. In the year 1977, whom did Joseph P. Teasdale succeed as the Governor of Missouri?
Kit Bond

419. Name any one award Rex Tillerson received in the year 2012.
Order of Friendship

420. Where was Zell Miller, a Democratic senator from Georgia, born?
Young Harris

421. Can you name the politician who received the «Mount Holyoke College Mary Lyon Award» in the year 2001?
Mona Sutphen

422. George Voinovich became a senator in the year 2007. Which state did he represent?
Ohio

423. Name any one award Antonia Novello received in the year 1994.
National Women's Hall of Fame

424. Can you name the politician who received the «Leo Szilard Lectureship Award» in the year 1995?
Roald Sagdeev

425. What is the name of David René de Rothschild's father?
Guy de Rothschild

426. Claire McCaskill became a senator in the year 2015. Which state did she represent?
Missouri

427. Jon Tester became a senator in the year 2013. Which state did he represent?
Montana

428. In which year did Jane Harman marry Sidney Harman?
1980

429. In the year 1978, Hillary Clinton worked as a board member in which nonprofit organization?
Legal Services Corporation

430. Ben Cardin, who belonged to the Democratic Party, became a senator in the year 2009. Which state did he represent?
Maryland

431. Bill Frist became a senator in the year 1997. Which state did he represent?
Tennessee

432. Patrick Leahy became a US senator from Vermont in the year 2015. Where was he born?
Montpelier

433. Can you name the politician who received the «Sagamore of the Wabash» award in the year 1989?
John R. Gregg

434. From which university did Joe Biden get his Juris Doctor degree in law?
Syracuse University College of Law

435. Name any one award Madeleine Albright received in the year 2010.
Colorado Women's Hall of Fame

436. Name any one award Yehudi Menuhin received in the year 1997.
Princess of Asturias Award for Concord

437. Pat Roberts became a senator in the year 1997. Which state did he represent?
Kansas

438. What is the name of Mitt Romney's mother?
Lenore Romney

439. Who wrote the book «Hard Choices»?
Hillary Clinton

440. From which university did Boyd K. Rutherford get his bachelor's degree in economics?
Howard University

441. Where did David McKinley get his Bachelor of Engineering degree in civil engineering from?
Purdue University

442. Claire McCaskill became a US senator from Missouri in the year 2011. Where was she born?
Rolla

443. Who had hired Alex X. Mooney as a member of congressional staff in the year 1993?
Roscoe Bartlett

444. What is the name of Skip Humphrey's mother?
Muriel Humphrey Brown

445. Can you name the politician who received the «Catalonia International Prize» in the year 2010?
Jimmy Carter

446. Judd Gregg became a US senator from New Hampshire in the year 1995. Where was he born?
Nashua

447. Name any one award Dan Burton received in the year 1999.
James Madison Award

448. Name any one award John Lewis received in the year 2001.
Profile in Courage Award

449. Can you name the politician who received the «Woodrow Wilson Awards» in the year 2012?
Hillary Clinton

450. Can you name the politician who received the «Theodore Roosevelt Award» in the year 1992?
Jack Kemp

451. Who replaced Tim Hutchinson as the senator from Arkansas in the year 1997?
Mark Pryor

452. Who had hired Judy Biggert as Clerk in the year 1963?
Luther Merritt Swygert

453. From which university did Walter Maddox get his bachelor's degree in political science?
University of Alabama at Birmingham

454. Name any one award Pete Stark received in the year 2008.
Humanist of the Year

455. Where was Jon Tester, a Democratic senator from Montana, born?
Havre

456. Name any one award Lyndon B. Johnson received in the year 1965.
Lasker-Bloomberg Public Service Award

457. What medal did John F. Kennedy get in the year 1945?
American Campaign Medal

458. Where was Bill Cassidy, a Republican senator from Louisiana, born?
Highland Park

459. Whom did Pete Buttigieg marry in the year 2018?
Chasten Buttigieg

460. In the year 1994, Henry McMaster worked as a chairperson in which political party?
South Carolina Republican Party

461. John McCain became a senator in the year 2003. Which state did he represent?
Arizona

462. Name any one award Bella Abzug received in the year 1994.
National Women's Hall of Fame

463. Jim Risch became a US senator from Idaho in the year 2011. Where was he born?
Milwaukee

464. Where was Pat Roberts, a Republican senator from Kansas, born?

Topeka

465. Where was Joe Manchin, a Democratic senator from West Virginia, born?
Farmington

466. Name any one award Rosalynn Carter received in the year 2005.
Women's Caucus for Art Lifetime Achievement Award

467. Who had hired Kevin McCarthy as a member of congressional staff in the year 1987?
Bill Thomas

468. Dan Quayle became a US senator from Indiana in the year 1981. Where was he born?
Indianapolis

469. In which year did Mark Parkinson become the Governor of Kansas?
2009

470. Thad Cochran, who belonged to the Republican Party, became a senator in the year 2011. Which state did he represent?
Mississippi

471. Name any one award Henry Kissinger received in the year 1972.
Time Person of the Year

472. Jim Webb became a senator in the year 2007. Which state did he represent?
Virginia

473. Whom did Tony Knowles replace as the mayor of Anchorage in the year 1982?

474. Daniel S. Sullivan, who belonged to the Republican Party, became a senator in the year 2015. Which state did he represent?
Alaska

475. Who had hired Richard Blumenthal as a law clerk in the year 1974?
Harry Blackmun

476. In which year did Bob Riley become the Governor of Alabama?
2003

477. Jim Mountain Inhofe became a US senator from Oklahoma in the year 2011. Where was he born?
Des Moines

478. Can you name the politician who received the «Anisfield-Wolf Book Awards» in the year 1964?
Daniel Patrick Moynihan

479. Can you name the politician who received the «EFF Pioneer Award» in the year 2011?
Ron Lee Wyden

480. Name any one award Bob Mathias received in the year 1995.
Theodore Roosevelt Award

481. Mike Crapo became a US senator from Idaho in the year 2005. Where was he born?
Bonneville County

482. Joe Lieberman became a US senator from Connecticut in the year 2009. Where was he born?

Stamford

483. John Breaux became a senator in the year 1997. Which state did he represent?
Louisiana

484. Donald Stewart became a US senator from Alabama in the year 1978. Where was he born?
Munford

485. Name any one award John C. Whitehead received in the year 1987.
Freedom Award

486. Can you name the politician who received the «Honorary doctorate of the University of South Carolina» award in the year 2015?
Nikki Haley

487. Mark Kirk, who belonged to the Republican Party, became a senator in the year 2015. Which state did he represent?
Illinois

488. Carl Levin became a senator in the year 1979. Which state did he represent?
Michigan

489. From which university did Rex Tillerson get his Bachelor of Science degree in civil engineering?
University of Texas at Austin

490. Judd Gregg became a US senator from New Hampshire in the year 2003. Where was he born?
Nashua

491. Name any one award Tim Kaine received in the year

2017.
Grand Cross of the Order of Isabella the Catholic

492. In which year did Mark Dayton become the Governor of Minnesota?
2011

493. Can you name the politician who received the «Charlemagne Prize» in the year 1959?
George Marshall

494. Can you name the politician who received the «David Livingstone Centenary Medal» in the year 1917?
Theodore Roosevelt

495. Name any one award Ayaan Hirsi Ali received in the year 2004.
Dutchman of the Year

496. John McCain became a senator in the year 2017. Which state did he represent?
Arizona

497. Where was Elizabeth Dole, a Republican senator from North Carolina, born?
Salisbury

498. Name any one award Peter J. Brennan received in the year 2005.
Labor Hall of Honor

499. Who had hired Sean Spicer as White House Press Secretary in the year 2017?
Donald Trump

500. Where was Bob Packwood, a Republican senator from Oregon, born?

Portland

501. Whom did Mark Udall replace as the senator from Colorado in the year 2009?
Wayne Allard

502. Can you name the politician who received the «Michigan Women's Hall of Fame» award in the year 2015?
Candice Miller

503. Who had hired Barbara Lee as a member of congressional staff in the year 1975?
Ron Dellums

504. In the year 2005, Elizabeth Cheney worked as Assistant Secretary of State for Near Eastern Affairs in which foreign affairs ministry?
United States Department of State

505. Can you name the politician who received the «Lasker-Bloomberg Public Service Award» in the year 2000?
Betty Ford

506. Can you name the politician who received the «doctor honoris causa» award in the year 1993?
Hillary Clinton

507. Name any one award Bill Clinton received in the year 2006.
Fulbright Prize

508. J. Bennett Johnston, Jr. became a US senator from Louisiana in the year 1993. Where was he born?
Shreveport

509. From which university did Michelle Obama get her Bachelor of Arts degree in sociology?
Princeton University

510. Where did Jay Rockefeller work as a chancellor in the year 1973?
West Virginia Wesleyan College

511. Name any one award John Netherland Heiskell received in the year 1958.
Elijah Parish Lovejoy Award

512. Lindsey Graham, who belonged to the Republican Party, became a senator in the year 2017. Which state did he represent?
South Carolina

513. What is the name of Gavin Newsom's father?
William Newsom

514. In the year 1973, whom did Thomas P. Salmon succeed as the Governor of Vermont?
Deane C. Davis

515. Name any one award Yehudi Menuhin received in the year 1996.
Gramophone Award for Lifetime Achievement

516. Whom did Bob Graham marry in the year 1959?
Adele Khoury Graham

517. In which year did Ron DeSantis marry Casey DeSantis?
2010

518. Name any one award George P. Shultz received in the year 2010.

519. Whom did Jim Webb marry in the year 2006?
Hong Le Webb

520. Spencer Abraham became a US senator from Michigan in the year 1997. Where was he born?
East Lansing

521. Can you name the politician who received the «Francis Boyer Award» in the year 1981?
Henry Kissinger

522. What medal did John W. Gardner get in the year 1966?
Public Welfare Medal

523. Who replaced Robert C. Smith as the senator from New Hampshire in the year 1990?
John E. Sununu

524. Can you name the politician who received the «Nobel Peace Prize» in the year 1953?
George Marshall

525. Richard Shelby, who belonged to the Democratic Party, became a senator in the year 1991. Which state did he represent?
Alabama

526. Deb Fischer, who belonged to the Republican Party, became a senator in the year 2017. Which state did she represent?
Nebraska

527. Name any one award Lawrence Summers received in the year 1985.

Fellow of the Econometric Society

528. Can you name the politician who received the «Presidential Medal of Freedom» in the year 2013?
Richard Lugar

529. Can you name the politician who received the «Sidney Powers Memorial Award» in the year 2011?
John W. Shelton

530. What is the name of Valerie Jarrett's father?
James E. Bowman

531. Name any one award Cecilia Muñoz received in the year 2000.
MacArthur Fellows Program

532. In which year did Jim Risch marry Vicki Risch?
1968

533. Name any one award Vern Ehlers received in the year 2002.
AAAS Philip Hauge Abelson Prize

534. Where did Arnold Schwarzenegger get his Bachelor of Arts degree in administration from?
University of Wisconsin–Superior

535. John V. Tunney became a senator in the year 1971. Which state did he represent?
California

536. Kent Conrad became a US senator from North Dakota in the year 2011. Where was he born?
Bismarck

537. In which year did Mark S. Schweiker become the

Governor of Pennsylvania?
2001

538. Can you name the politician who received the «Library of Congress Prize for American Fiction» in the year 2009?
John Grisham

539. Who replaced John Breaux as the senator from Louisiana in the year 1987?
David Vitter

540. Can you name the politician who received the «Maryland Women's Hall of Fame» award in the year 2015?
Beverly Byron

541. In which year did Maggie Hassan become the Governor of New Hampshire?
2013

542. In the year 2011, whom did Peter Shumlin succeed as the Governor of Vermont?
Jim Douglas

543. Where was Mark Begich, a senator from Alaska, born?
Anchorage

544. Who replaced John Heinz as the senator from Pennsylvania in the year 1977?
Harris Wofford

545. Jeanne Shaheen became a US senator from New Hampshire in the year 2011. Where was she born?
St. Charles

546. From which university did Giorgos Kaminis get his bachelor's degree in jurisprudence?
National and Kapodistrian University of Athens

547. What is the name of Cameron Kerry's father?
Richard J. Kerry

548. Whom did Michelle Obama marry in the year 1992?
Barack Obama

549. Name any one award Corliss Lamont received in the year 1977.
Humanist of the Year

550. Name any one award Mary Beck received in the year 1991.
Michigan Women's Hall of Fame

551. Name any one award Ilhan Omar received in the year 2017.
OkayAfrica 100 Women

552. Name any one award Lawrence Summers received in the year 2000.
Golden Plate Award

553. Richard M. Burr became a senator in the year 2015. Which state did he represent?
North Carolina

554. David Durenberger became a US senator from Minnesota in the year 1993. Where was he born?
St. Cloud

555. Can you name the politician who received the «National Women's Hall of Fame» award in the year 1973?
Mary McLeod Bethune

556. Can you name the politician who received the «Nobel Peace Prize» in the year 1973?
Henry Kissinger

557. What is the name of Gwen Graham's father?
Bob Graham

558. What medal did Russell E. Train receive in the year 1981?
Public Welfare Medal

559. In which year did Juan Francisco Luis become the Governor of the United States Virgin Islands?
1978

560. Name any one award Constance Baker Motley received in the year 1993.
National Women's Hall of Fame

561. Spencer Abraham became a US senator from Michigan in the year 1995. Where was he born?
East Lansing

562. What medal did Edward Brooke receive in the year 1967?
Spingarn Medal

563. Name any one award Hillary Clinton received in the year 1998.
Gallup's most admired man and woman poll

564. Kirsten Gillibrand became a senator in the year 2015. Which state did she represent?
New York

565. In which year did John Engler become the Governor

of Michigan?
1991

566. Whom did Robert J. Bentley marry in the year 1965?
Dianne Jones

567. Can you name the politician who received the «Heinrich Mann Prize» in the year 1953?
Stefan Heym

568. Where did Peggy Flanagan get her bachelor's degree in child psychology from?
University of Minnesota

569. Tom Cotton became a US senator from Arkansas in the year 2015. Where was he born?
Dardanelle

570. Can you name the politician who received the «Fulbright Prize» in the year 2004?
Colin Powell

571. Tim Johnson became a senator in the year 2007. Which state did he represent?
South Dakota

572. Name any one award J. Lister Hill received in the year 1968.
Lasker-Bloomberg Public Service Award

573. Can you name the politician who received the «Lasker-Bloomberg Public Service Award» in the year 1973?
Warren Grant Magnuson

574. Where did Jerry Moran work as the president in the year 1994?

575. Can you name the politician who received the «Rumford Prize» in the year 2008?
George P. Shultz

576. Who became the mayor of Madison in the year 1973?
Paul Soglin

577. In the year 1993, whom did Mike Lowry succeed as the Governor of Washington?
Booth Gardner

578. Can you name the politician who received the «Freedom Award» in the year 2005?
Bill Clinton

579. Jim Bunning became a senator in the year 2009. Which state did he represent?
Kentucky

580. Hank Brown, who belonged to the Republican Party, became a senator in the year 1993. Which state did he represent?
Colorado

581. Whom did Walter Capps marry in the year 1960?
Lois Capps

582. What medal did George H. W. Bush get in the year 2014?
Robert Schuman Medal

583. Name any one award Al Smith received in the year 2006.
Labor Hall of Honor

584. Can you name the politician who received the «Ellis Island Medal of Honor» in the year 1986?
Donald Trump

585. In the year 1992, whom did Jim Guy Tucker succeed as the Governor of Arkansas?
Bill Clinton

586. Can you name the politician who received the «Daniel Patrick Moynihan Prize» in the year 2012?
Paul Volcker

587. Can you name the politician who received the «Albert Medal» in the year 1941?
Franklin Delano Roosevelt

588. In the year 2003, whom did Mark Sanford succeed as the Governor of South Carolina?
Jim Hodges

589. Name any one award Sharpe James received in the year 2005.
New Jersey Mayors Hall of Fame

590. Can you name the politician who received the «Eisenmann Medal» in the year 2002?
William S. Clark

591. Can you name the politician who received the «Nobel Prize in Economics» in the year 1978?
Herbert A. Simon

592. Name any one award Tom Bradley received in the year 1977.
Theodore Roosevelt Award

593. Who had hired Robert Gibbs as White House Press

Secretary in the year 2009?
Barack Obama

594. Name any one award Maggie Kuhn received in the year 1978.
Humanist of the Year

595. Where was John Neely Kennedy, a Republican senator from Louisiana, born?
Centreville

596. What is the name of Mike Pence's father?
Edward J. Pence, Jr.

597. Johnny Isakson became a US senator from Georgia in the year 2015. Where was he born?
Atlanta

598. Whom did Jon Lynn Christensen marry in the year 1998?
Tara Dawn Holland

599. Whom did John R. McKernan marry in the year 1989?
Olympia Snowe

600. Who wrote the book «Patriotism of the American Jew»?
Samuel Walker McCall

601. Can you name the politician who received the «Theodore Roosevelt Award» in the year 2010?
George John Mitchell Jr.

602. Where was Rod Grams, a senator from Minnesota, born?
Princeton

603. Can you name the politician who received the «National Women's Hall of Fame» award in the year 2001?
Rosalynn Carter

604. Can you name the politician who received the «Golden Brain Award» in the year 2000?
Frederick Miles

605. Where was Roy Blunt, a Republican senator from Missouri, born?
Niangua

606. What is the name of George W. Bush's father?
George H. W. Bush

607. Can you name the politician who received the «Spingarn Medal» in the year 1991?
Colin Powell

608. Name any one award Hattie Caraway received in the year 2001.
Distinguished Americans series

609. Name any one award William Everett Potter received in the year 1997.
Disney Legends

610. Who wrote the book «The Caged Virgin»?
Ayaan Hirsi Ali

611. Tim Johnson became a senator in the year 2001. Which state did he represent?
South Dakota

612. In which year did Matt Blunt become the Governor of Missouri?
2005

613. In which year did Paul Cellucci become the Governor of Massachusetts?
1999

614. Who wrote the book «Trump: The Art of the Deal»?
Donald Trump

615. In the year 1997, whom did Jane Dee Hull succeed as the Governor of Arizona?
Fife Symington III

616. What is the name of Ben Carson's father?
Robert Solomon Carson

617. In the year 2003, whom did Rod Blagojevich succeed as the Governor of Illinois?
George Ryan

618. Russ Feingold became a US senator from Wisconsin in the year 2001. Where was he born?
Janesville

619. Don Nickles, who belonged to the Republican Party, became a senator in the year 1997. Which state did he represent?
Oklahoma

620. Where was Carol Moseley Braun, a Democratic senator from Illinois, born?
Chicago

621. Tina Smith, who belonged to the Democratic Party, became a senator in the year 2018. Which state did she represent?
Minnesota

622. Where was William L. Armstrong, a senator from Colorado, born?
Fremont

623. Can you name the politician who received the «Ernst Reuter Medal» in the year 1980?
Yehudi Menuhin

624. In which year did Earl Ray Tomblin become the Governor of West Virginia?
2010

625. Bob P. Casey, Jr. became a US senator from Pennsylvania in the year 2015. Where was he born?
Scranton

626. What is the name of David Miliband's mother?
Marion Kozak

627. In which year did Kay Bailey Hutchison marry Ray Hutchison?
1978

628. Can you name the politician who received the «United Nations Peace Medal» in the year 1973?
Dixy Lee Ray

629. Barack Obama became a US senator from Illinois in the year 2005. Where was he born?
Kapiolani Medical Center for Women and Children

630. Where did Hillary Clinton work as a board member in the year 1985?
TCBY

631. Can you name the politician who received the «Medal of quality government's knighf» in the year 2017?

632. In the year 1988, whom did Ray Mabus succeed as the Governor of Mississippi?
William Allain

633. Trent Lott became a US senator from Mississippi in the year 1995. Where was he born?
Grenada

634. Bob Bennett became a US senator from Utah in the year 1995. Where was he born?
Salt Lake City

635. In which year did Buddy Roemer become the Governor of Louisiana?
1988

636. Who had hired George Nethercutt as a member of chief of staff in the year 1972?
Ted Stevens

637. Who had hired Daniel Lipinski as a member of congressional staff in the year 1995?
Jerry Costello

638. Lindsey Graham became a senator in the year 2013. Which state did he represent?
South Carolina

639. What is the name of Michael Bloomberg's mother?
Charlotte Bloomberg

640. Thomas Rolland Tillis became a US senator from North Carolina in the year 2015. Where was he born?
Jacksonville

641. Kent Conrad became a senator in the year 2001. Which state did he represent?
North Dakota

642. Sheldon Whitehouse became a senator in the year 2007. Which state did he represent?
Rhode Island

643. Name any one award Donald Trump received in the year 1990.
Golden Raspberry Award for Worst Supporting Actor

644. What is the name of Ted Mondale's mother?
Joan Mondale

645. Name any one award Ronald Reagan received in the year 1988.
Francis Boyer Award

646. Name any one award Barbara Bush received in the year 1997.
Harold W. McGraw Prize in Education

647. In which year did Tim Kaine become the Governor of Virginia?
2006

648. Name any one award Albert II received in the year 2006.
Grand Cross of the Legion of Honour

649. Joe Lieberman became a senator in the year 1999. Which state did he represent?
Connecticut

650. Where did Charlene Drew Jarvis get her Master of Science degree in psychology from?

651. Maggie Hassan became a US senator from New Hampshire in the year 2017. Where was she born?
Boston

652. Name any one award Zoe Lofgren received in the year 2014.
EFF Pioneer Award

653. Jeff Sessions became a senator in the year 1999. Which state did he represent?
Alabama

654. Can you name the politician who received the «Spingarn Medal» in the year 1942?
A. Philip Randolph

655. Who had hired Richard Blumenthal as a secretary in the year 1975?
Abraham A. Ribicoff

656. Who replaced Thad Cochran as the senator from Mississippi in the year 1978?
Cindy Hyde-Smith

657. Name any one award Martha Griffiths received in the year 1983.
Michigan Women's Hall of Fame

658. Can you name the politician who received the «Hilal-e-Pakistan» award in the year 2008?
Richard Lugar

659. Kelly Ayotte became a senator in the year 2011. Which state did she represent?
New Hampshire

660. Max Cleland, who belonged to the Democratic Party, became a senator in the year 2001. Which state did he represent?
Georgia

661. Rick Santorum became a senator in the year 2001. Which state did he represent?
Pennsylvania

662. Richard Lugar, who belonged to the Republican Party, became a senator in the year 1993. Which state did he represent?
Indiana

663. Where did Rob Astorino get his Bachelor of Arts degree in communication studies from?
Fordham University

664. In which year did David Walters become the Governor of Oklahoma?
1991

665. Name any one award Hillary Clinton received in the year 2004.
doctor honoris causa

666. Jeanne Shaheen, who belonged to the Democratic Party, became a senator in the year 2013. Which state did she represent?
New Hampshire

667. Bernie Sanders became a senator in the year 2015. Which state did he represent?
Vermont

668. Can you name the politician who received the

«Michigan Women's Hall of Fame» award in the year 1997?
Matilda Dodge Wilson

669. In which year did James Blanchard become the Governor of Michigan?
1983

670. Jeff Bingaman, who belonged to the Democratic Party, became a senator in the year 2003. Which state did he represent?
New Mexico

671. Can you name the politician who received the «Doublespeak Award» in the year 2007?
Alberto Gonzales

672. Who had hired Jo Bonner as an employee in the year 1985?
Sonny Callahan

673. What medal did Stewart Udall receive in the year 1967?
Audubon Medal

674. What is the name of Beto O'Rourke's mother?
Melissa O'Rourke

675. Martin Heinrich became a senator in the year 2013. Which state did he represent?
New Mexico

676. Whom did Mary Bono marry in the year 1986?
Sonny Bono

677. Tom Carper became a US senator from Delaware in the year 2009. Where was he born?

Beckley

678. Name any one award Herbert A. Simon received in the year 1975.
Turing Award

679. In the year 1996, whom did Mike Huckabee succeed as the Governor of Arkansas?
Jim Guy Tucker

680. In the year 2004, Nancy Keenan was the president of which organization?
NARAL Pro-Choice America

681. Name any one award Barack Obama received in the year 2016.
German Media Award

682. Name any one award Gerald Ford received in the year 1975.
Theodore Roosevelt Award

683. Whom did Sonny Bono marry in the year 1964?
Cher

684. Name any one award Lucius D. Clay received in the year 1965.
Grand Cross 1st class of the Order of Merit of the Federal Republic of Germany

685. Harry Reid, who belonged to the Democratic Party, became a senator in the year 2003. Which state did he represent?
Nevada

686. Name any one award Ramsey Clark received in the year 1992.

687. In the year 2002, whom did John O. Bennett succeed as the Governor of New Jersey?
John Farmer

688. Name any one award Dwight D. Eisenhower received in the year 1961.
Horatio Alger Award

689. Name any one award Walter Mondale received in the year 2008.
Order of the Paulownia Flowers

690. Name any one award Percy Sutton received in the year 1992.
Candace Award

691. Can you name the politician who received the «James Madison Award» in the year 2012?
Zoe Lofgren

692. Name any one award Margaret Chase Smith received in the year 1973.
National Women's Hall of Fame

693. Jim Mountain Inhofe became a US senator from Oklahoma in the year 2001. Where was he born?
Des Moines

694. In which year did Steve Henry marry Heather French Henry?
2000

695. Name any one award Herbert A. Simon received in the year 1984.
Josiah Willard Gibbs Lectureship

696. Where did Virginia Foxx work as the president in the year 1987?
Mayland Community College

697. In the year 1974, Mitch McConnell worked as United States Assistant Attorney General in which government agency?
U.S. Department of Justice Office of Legislative Affairs

698. Can you name the politician who received the «Thomas Merton Award» in the year 1974?
Dick Gregory

699. Dick Durbin, who belonged to the Democratic Party, became a senator in the year 1999. Which state did he represent?
Illinois

700. Where was Conrad Burns, a Republican senator from Montana, born?
Gallatin

701. What is the name of William Scranton III's father?
William Scranton

702. Charles Ellis Schumer, who belonged to the Democratic Party, became a senator in the year 2013. Which state did he represent?
New York

703. In which year did John McCain marry Cindy McCain?
1980

704. Can you name the politician who received the «Sam Adams Award» in the year 2002?
Coleen Rowley

705. Can you name the politician who received the «honorary doctor of Harvard University» award in the year 2015?
Deval Patrick

706. Who wrote the book «The Curse of Lono»?
Hunter S. Thompson

707. In which year did Jim McGreevey become the Governor of New Jersey?
2002

708. In the year 1985, whom did John Ashcroft succeed as the Governor of Missouri?
Kit Bond

709. Can you name the politician who received the «National Women's Hall of Fame» award in the year 2000?
Janet Reno

710. Name any one award Al Gore received in the year 2005.
Webby Lifetime Achievement Award

711. Name any one award Newt Gingrich received in the year 1997.
Doublespeak Award

712. Where was Richard Shelby, a Republican senator from Alabama, born?
Birmingham

713. Whom did John Kasich marry in the year 1975?
Mary Lee Griffith

714. Where was Saxby Chambliss, a Republican senator

from Georgia, born?
Warrenton

715. Pete Domenici became a senator in the year 1995. Which state did he represent?
New Mexico

716. Can you name the politician who received the «Gandhi Peace Award» in the year 2003?
Dennis Kucinich

717. Can you name the politician who received the «Time 100» award in the year 2012?
Hillary Clinton

718. Whom did Bill Paxon marry in the year 1994?
Susan Molinari

719. Where was John Edwards, a Democratic senator from North Carolina, born?
Seneca

720. In which year did Carlos S. Camacho become the Governor of the Northern Mariana Islands?
1978

721. Where did Tom Campbell get his Doctor of Philosophy degree in economics from?
University of Chicago

722. Name any one award Cora Brown received in the year 1992.
Michigan Women's Hall of Fame

723. Can you name the politician who received the «Chicago Gay and Lesbian Hall of Fame» award in the year 2001?

Sara Feigenholtz

724. Name any one award Patricia Schroeder received in the year 1985.
Colorado Women's Hall of Fame

725. In which year did Carlos Romero Barceló become the Governor of Puerto Rico?
1977

726. In which year did Howard Dean marry Judith Steinberg Dean?
1981

727. Can you name the politician who received the «member of the Alabama Academy of Honor» award in the year 1969?
George Wallace

728. Can you name the politician who received the «Hoover Medal» in the year 1945?
William Henry Harrison

729. In which year did Andrew Cuomo marry Kerry Kennedy?
1990

730. John Seymour became a senator in the year 1991. Which state did he represent?
California

731. Can you name the politician who received the «Knight Grand Cross of the Order of the Bath» award in the year 1943?
Dwight D. Eisenhower

732. In the year 1977, whom did Jay Rockefeller succeed

as the Governor of West Virginia?
Arch A. Moore

733. Kit Bond became a US senator from Missouri in the year 2001. Where was he born?
St. Louis

734. In which year did Juan Babauta become the Governor of the Northern Mariana Islands?
2002

735. Can you name the politician who received the «Theodore Roosevelt Award» in the year 1967?
Dwight D. Eisenhower

736. Can you name the politician who received the «Foreign Member of the Royal Society» award in the year 2014?
Steven Chu

737. Lisa Murkowski became a US senator from Alaska in the year 2015. Where was she born?
Ketchikan

738. Whom did Gary Locke marry in the year 1994?
Mona Lee Locke

739. Chuck Grassley, who belonged to the Republican Party, became a senator in the year 1991. Which state did he represent?
Iowa

740. Whom did Dan Coats replace as the senator from Indiana in the year 2011?
Evan Bayh

741. In the year 1999, whom did Mike Johanns succeed as

the Governor of Nebraska?
Ben Nelson

742. In the year 2011, whom did John Kitzhaber succeed as the Governor of Oregon?
Ted Kulongoski

743. Carl Levin, who belonged to the Democratic Party, became a senator in the year 2005. Which state did he represent?
Michigan

744. In the year 2004, whom did Jodi Rell succeed as the Governor of Connecticut?
John G. Rowland

745. What is the name of Gavin Newsom's mother?
Tessa Newsom

746. Lamar Alexander, who belonged to the Republican Party, became a senator in the year 2015. Which state did he represent?
Tennessee

747. What is the name of Martin O'Malley's father?
Thomas Martin O'Malley

748. Name any one award Herbert A. Simon received in the year 1993.
APA Award for Lifetime Contributions to Psychology

749. Ken Salazar became a senator in the year 2007. Which state did he represent?
Colorado

750. Name any one award Richard Lugar received in the year 2017.

751. Whom did Alan K. Simpson replace as the senator from Wyoming in the year 1979?
Clifford Hansen

752. Maria Cantwell became a senator in the year 2011. Which state did she represent?
Washington

753. Who became the mayor of Manchester in the year 2010?
Ted Gatsas

754. George Allen became a US senator from Virginia in the year 2001. Where was he born?
Whittier

755. Who replaced Jim Jeffords as the senator from Vermont in the year 1989?
Bernie Sanders

756. Name any one award Dale Bumpers received in the year 1995.
Maxwell Finland Award

757. In the year 1989, Nancy Keenan worked as a superintendent in which state education agency?
Montana Office of Public Instruction

758. Can you name the politician who received the «honorary doctor of the University of Edinburgh» award in the year 2016?
Albert II

759. Where was Jim DeMint, a Republican senator from South Carolina, born?

Greenville

760. In which year did George Ryan become the Governor of Illinois?
1999

761. In which year did Newt Gingrich marry Callista Gingrich?
2000

762. What medal did Nancy Reagan receive in the year 2002?
Presidential Medal of Freedom

763. What is the name of John P. Daley's father?
Richard J. Daley

764. Patrick Leahy, who belonged to the Democratic Party, became a senator in the year 2005. Which state did he represent?
Vermont

765. In which year did Scott Walker become the Governor of Wisconsin?
2011

766. Name any one award Frank B. Kellogg received in the year 1929.
Nobel Peace Prize

767. Can you name the politician who received the «Presidential Citizens Medal» in the year 2001?
Fred Shuttlesworth

768. Can you name the politician who received the «Chicago Gay and Lesbian Hall of Fame» award in the year 2005?

Carol Ronen

769. Who replaced Malcolm Wallop as the senator from Wyoming in the year 1977?
Craig L. Thomas

770. Can you name the politician who received the «Global Economy Prize» in the year 2011?
Lawrence Summers

771. What is the name of Arnold Schwarzenegger's mother?
Aurelia Schwarzenegger

772. Can you name the politician who received the «EFF Pioneer Award» in the year 2016?
Mark Leno

773. Name any one award Miguel d'Escoto Brockmann received in the year 1987.
Thomas Merton Award

774. What is the name of Jay Rockefeller's mother?
Blanchette Ferry Rockefeller

775. Can you name the politician who received the «California Hall of Fame» award in the year 2008?
Leland Stanford

776. Can you name the politician who received the «Thomas Merton Award» in the year 2009?
Dennis Kucinich

777. In which year did Lincoln Chafee become the Governor of Rhode Island?
2011

778. Can you name the politician who received the «National Defense Service Medal» in the year 1966?
Dwight D. Eisenhower

779. Jim Sasser became a US senator from Tennessee in the year 1991. Where was he born?
Memphis

780. Can you name the politician who received the «Champions of the Earth» award in the year 2008?
Albert II

781. Kay Bailey Hutchison became a senator in the year 2007. Which state did she represent?
Texas

782. Roy Blunt became a senator in the year 2013. Which state did he represent?
Missouri

783. Can you name the politician who received the «Albert Einstein Peace Prize» in the year 1981?
George F. Kennan

784. In the year 2005, whom did John Lynch succeed as the Governor of New Hampshire?
Craig Benson

785. Name any one award Gary Locke received in the year 2006.
honorary doctor of the Peking University

786. Olympia Snowe, who belonged to the Republican Party, became a senator in the year 2001. Which state did she represent?
Maine

787. What is the name of Joseph P. Kennedy II's mother?
Ethel Skakel Kennedy

788. Alan K. Simpson, who belonged to the Republican Party, became a senator in the year 1993. Which state did he represent?
Wyoming

789. Where was Charles Ellis Schumer, a Democratic senator from New York, born?
Brooklyn

790. Name any one award Thomas M. Storke received in the year 1962.
Elijah Parish Lovejoy Award

791. Debbie Stabenow became a senator in the year 2005. Which state did she represent?
Michigan

792. Ted Kennedy became a US senator from Massachusetts in the year 1993. Where was he born?
Boston

793. Harrison Schmitt became a senator in the year 1977. Which state did he represent?
New Mexico

794. Can you name the politician who received the «Doublespeak Award» in the year 1997?
Bill Clinton

795. Whom did Eliot Spitzer marry in the year 1987?
Silda Wall Spitzer

796. Charles Ellis Schumer became a US senator from New York in the year 1999. Where was he born?

Brooklyn

797. Can you name the politician who received the «Pulitzer Prize for Biography or Autobiography» in the year 1957?
John F. Kennedy

798. Catherine Cortez Masto became a US senator from Nevada in the year 2017. Where was she born?
Las Vegas

799. Sam Nunn became a senator in the year 1972. Which state did he represent?
Georgia

800. Can you name the politician who received the «Erik Bye's Memorial Prize» in the year 2008?
Cindy Sheehan

801. Can you name the politician who received the «honorary doctor of the University of St Andrews» award in the year 2013?
Hillary Clinton

802. What is the name of Pete Buttigieg's father?
Joseph Buttigieg

803. Who replaced David Vitter as the senator from Louisiana in the year 2005?
John Neely Kennedy

804. In the year 1977, Eddie Bernice Johnson worked as an official in which ministry?
United States Department of Health, Education, and Welfare

805. Mark Udall became a US senator from Colorado in the year 2011. Where was he born?

Tucson

806. Can you name the politician who received the «Labor Hall of Honor» award in the year 1996?
William Green

807. Who replaced Bill Frist as the senator from Tennessee in the year 1995?
Bob Corker

808. Can you name the politician who received the «Elizabeth Blackwell Award» in the year 1991?
Antonia Novello

809. In which year did John Delaney marry April McClain?
1990

810. Who wrote the book «Heretic: Why Islam Needs a Reformation Now»?
Ayaan Hirsi Ali

811. Can you name the politician who received the «Virtuti Militari» award in the year 1944?
Dwight D. Eisenhower

812. Name any one award Belva Ann Lockwood received in the year 1983.
National Women's Hall of Fame

813. In which year did Ted Strickland become the Governor of Ohio?
2007

814. Whom did Ileana Ros-Lehtinen marry in the year 1984?
Dexter Lehtinen

815. Where did Mary Jo White get her Juris Doctor degree in law from?
Columbia Law School

816. Who replaced Rick Santorum as the senator from Pennsylvania in the year 1995?
Bob P. Casey, Jr.

817. Whom did Al Franken replace as the senator from Minnesota in the year 2009?
Norm Coleman

818. Where was Chuck Hagel, a Republican senator from Nebraska, born?
North Platte

819. In which year did Mike Beebe become the Governor of Arkansas?
2007

820. Where did Tony Tinderholt get his master's degree in educational leadership from?
Touro College

821. Can you name the politician who received the «Tyler Prize for Environmental Achievement» in the year 1978?
Russell E. Train

822. Peter Fitzgerald, who belonged to the Republican Party, became a senator in the year 2001. Which state did he represent?
Illinois

823. In which year did Arnold Schwarzenegger become the Governor of California?
2003

824. Can you name the politician who received the «Horatio Alger Award» in the year 1953?
Herbert Hoover

825. In which year did Olympia Snowe marry Peter T. Snowe?
1969

826. Can you name the politician who received the «Hoover Medal» in the year 1946?
Vannevar Bush

827. What medal did John Chafee receive in the year 1992?
Audubon Medal

828. Richard Bryan became a senator in the year 1995. Which state did he represent?
Nevada

829. Can you name the politician who received the «Labor Hall of Honor» award in the year 2017?
Ronald Reagan

830. Name any one award Fannie Lou Hamer received in the year 1993.
National Women's Hall of Fame

831. Jeff Sessions, who belonged to the Republican Party, became a senator in the year 2003. Which state did he represent?
Alabama

832. Whom did Brett Kavanaugh marry in the year 2004?
Ashley Estes Kavanaugh

833. Can you name the politician who received the

«Harold W. McGraw Prize in Education» in the year 1989?
Richard Riley

834. Roy Blunt became a senator in the year 2017. Which state did he represent?
Missouri

835. In which year did Tom Ridge become the Governor of Pennsylvania?
1995

836. Can you name the politician who received the «Nobel Prize in Physics» in the year 1997?
Steven Chu

837. Name any one award Ross Perot received in the year 1987.
Raoul Wallenberg Award

838. Can you name the politician who received the «Spingarn Medal» in the year 1962?
Robert C. Weaver

839. Jon Kyl became a US senator from Arizona in the year 2007. Where was he born?
Oakland

840. In which year did Katherine Zappone marry Ann Louise Gilligan?
2003

841. Who replaced Trent Lott as the senator from Mississippi in the year 1989?
Roger Wicker

842. Name any one award Nancy Pelosi received in the year 2013.

843. In the year 2007, whom did Bill Ritter succeed as the Governor of Colorado?
Bill Owens

844. Can you name the politician who received the «Doublespeak Award» in the year 1995?
Newt Gingrich

845. Name any one award Barbara Jordan received in the year 1984.
Texas Women's Hall of Fame

846. In which year did Ann Richards become the Governor of Texas?
1991

847. Whom did Paul LePage marry in the year 1984?
Ann DeRosby

848. What is the name of Jerry Brown's mother?
Bernice Layne Brown

849. Name any one award Douglas MacArthur received in the year 1932.
Order of the White Lion

850. Can you name the politician who received the «Spingarn Medal» in the year 1990?
Douglas Wilder

851. Debbie Stabenow, who belonged to the Democratic Party, became a senator in the year 2017. Which state did she represent?
Michigan

852. Can you name the politician who received the «Rachel Carson Award» in the year 2009?
Sally Jewell

853. What is the name of Ted Mondale's father?
Walter Mondale

854. Can you name the politician who received the «Order of the Paulownia Flowers» award in the year 2008?
Howard Baker

855. Bob Graham became a US senator from Florida in the year 2001. Where was he born?
Coral Gables

856. In which year did Sam Nunn marry Colleen O'Brien Nunn?
1965

857. What is the name of Mitt Romney's father?
George W. Romney

858. Where was Sam Nunn, a Democratic senator from Georgia, born?
Macon

859. Name any one award Albert II received in the year 2016.
German Maritime Award

860. In the year 2001, whom did Mike Easley succeed as the Governor of North Carolina?
Jim Hunt

861. John Thune became a senator in the year 2007. Which state did he represent?
South Dakota

862. Can you name the politician who received the «Harold Pender Award» in the year 1987?
Herbert A. Simon

863. Can you name the politician who received the «Hubbard Medal» in the year 1962?
John Glenn

864. In which year did Fred Thompson marry Jeri Kehn Thompson?
2002

865. Can you name the politician who received the «Buber-Rosenzweig-Medal» in the year 1989?
Yehudi Menuhin

866. Where did Sammuel Sanes get his master's degree in education consultancy from?
University of the Virgin Islands

867. In the year 1977, Jane Harman worked as a secretary in which government agency?
Executive Office of the President of the United States

868. Jim Jeffords became a senator in the year 2005. Which state did he represent?
Vermont

869. Harry Reid became a senator in the year 1987. Which state did he represent?
Nevada

870. Who wrote the book «It Takes a Village»?
Hillary Clinton

871. Name any one award Donald Trump received in the

year 2007.
star on Hollywood Walk of Fame

872. Charles Ellis Schumer became a US senator from New York in the year 2017. Where was he born?
Brooklyn

873. Name any one award Barbara Mikulski received in the year 2011.
National Women's Hall of Fame

874. Who replaced Lincoln Chafee as the senator from Rhode Island in the year 1999?
Sheldon Whitehouse

875. Can you name the politician who received the «Labor Hall of Honor» award in the year 2005?
Robert Wood Johnson II

876. In the year 2003, whom did Donald Carcieri succeed as the Governor of Rhode Island?
Lincoln Almond

877. Where was Judd Gregg, a Republican senator from New Hampshire, born?
Nashua

878. Whom did Bob Kasten replace as the senator from Wisconsin in the year 1981?
Gaylord Nelson

879. Where was Patty Murray, a Democratic senator from Washington, born?
Seattle

880. Can you name the politician who received the «Presidential Medal of Freedom» in the year 1993?

Ronald Reagan

881. In which year did Karen Pence marry Mike Pence?
1985

882. Where was Chuck Grassley, a Republican senator from Iowa, born?
New Hartford

883. Where was Elizabeth Warren, a Democratic senator from Massachusetts, born?
Oklahoma City

884. Name any one award Clarence Thomas received in the year 1998.
Doublespeak Award

885. Name any one award Don Jones received in the year 2008.
Clyde E. Fant Memorial Award

886. Can you name the politician who received the «Spingarn Medal» in the year 2009?
Julian Bond

887. Can you name the politician who received the «Gandhi Peace Award» in the year 1970?
Wayne Lyman Morse

888. What is the name of Corine Mauch's mother?
Ursula Mauch

889. From which college did Sean Spicer get his Bachelor of Arts degree in government?
Connecticut College

890. Whom did Jon Huntsman, Jr. marry in the year 1983?

Mary Kaye Huntsman

891. Can you name the politician who received the «National Women's Hall of Fame» award in the year 1976?
Abigail Adams

892. In the year 1979, whom did Paul McDonald Calvo succeed as the Governor of Guam?
Ricardo Bordallo

893. Whom did Chuck Hagel replace as the senator from Nebraska in the year 1997?
J. James Exon

894. Who replaced Kent Conrad as the senator from North Dakota in the year 1992?
Mary Kathryn Heitkamp

895. Where was John Cornyn, a Republican senator from Texas, born?
Houston

896. Earl Blumenauer worked as a member of which community college in the year 1975?
Portland Community College

897. Name any one award Gus Hall received in the year 1980.
Order of Friendship

898. Name any one award Maryann Mahaffey received in the year 1997.
Michigan Women's Hall of Fame

899. Can you name the politician who received the «Elizabeth Blackwell Award» in the year 1968?
Constance Baker Motley

900. Chris Dodd became a US senator from Connecticut in the year 1995. Where was he born?
Willimantic

901. What medal did Mary McLeod Bethune receive in the year 1935?
Spingarn Medal

902. Where was Mark Kirk, a senator from Illinois, born?
Champaign

903. In the year 2001, whom did Bob Holden succeed as the Governor of Missouri?
Roger B. Wilson

904. Name any one award Herbert A. Simon received in the year 1988.
John von Neumann Theory Prize

905. Bob P. Casey, Jr., who belonged to the Democratic Party, became a senator in the year 2007. Which state did he represent?
Pennsylvania

906. Can you name the politician who received the «Cameron Prize of the University of Edinburgh» in the year 1946?
Albert Szent-Györgyi

907. Carl Levin became a US senator from Michigan in the year 2009. Where was he born?
Detroit

908. Robert Torricelli became a US senator from New Jersey in the year 1997. Where was he born?
Paterson

909. Where was Steve Symms, a senator from Idaho, born?
Nampa

910. Wayne Allard became a US senator from Colorado in the year 2007. Where was he born?
Fort Collins

911. Name any one award Connie Binsfeld received in the year 1998.
Michigan Women's Hall of Fame

912. Name any one award Kellyanne Conway received in the year 2017.
Doublespeak Award

913. Can you name the politician who received the «Peace Prize of the German Book Trade» in the year 1982?
George F. Kennan

914. Name any one award Vannevar Bush received in the year 1954.
William Procter Prize for Scientific Achievement

915. Who became the mayor of Madison in the year 2011?
Paul Soglin

916. Debbie Stabenow became a senator in the year 2013. Which state did she represent?
Michigan

917. Can you name the politician who received the «Nobel Prize in Physiology or Medicine» in the year 1936?
Albert Szent-Györgyi

918. Can you name the politician who received the «Grand

Cross of the Order of Infante Dom Henri» award in the year 2003?
Frank Carlucci

919. Where was John Culver, a senator from Iowa, born?
Rochester

920. Chuck Hagel became a US senator from Nebraska in the year 1999. Where was he born?
North Platte

921. John F. Reed, who belonged to the Democratic Party, became a senator in the year 1999. Which state did he represent?
Rhode Island

922. Can you name the politician who received the «Eric-M.-Warburg-Award» in the year 1992?
Henry Kissinger

923. Jim Mountain Inhofe became a US senator from Oklahoma in the year 1999. Where was he born?
Des Moines

924. In the year 2003, whom did Ted Kulongoski succeed as the Governor of Oregon?
John Kitzhaber

925. Where was Herb Kohl, a Democratic senator from Wisconsin, born?
Milwaukee

926. What is the name of Laura Bush's father?
Harold Welch

927. Mark Dayton became a senator in the year 2003. Which state did he represent?

Minnesota

928. In which year did John W. Carlin become the Governor of Kansas?
1979

929. Name any one award Andrew Jackson received in the year 1984.
National Book Award for Nonfiction

930. Where was Mark Pryor, a Democratic senator from Arkansas, born?
Fayetteville

931. In which year did Bernie Sanders marry Deborah Shiling Messing?
1964

932. Can you name the politician who received the «Nobel Peace Prize» in the year 1945?
Cordell Hull

933. Whom did Nancy Brinker marry in the year 1981?
Norman E. Brinker

934. From which university did Giorgos Kaminis get his doctorate degree in jurisprudence?
Pantheon-Sorbonne University

935. From which university did A. Donald McEachin get his Master of Divinity degree in theology?
Virginia Union University

936. Name any one award Sandra Day O'Connor received in the year 1995.
National Women's Hall of Fame

937. What is the name of Hillary Clinton's father?
Hugh E. Rodham

938. In which year did Bernie Sanders marry Jane O'Meara Sanders?
1988

939. Name any one award Daniel Inouye received in the year 2011.
Order of the Paulownia Flowers

940. Jon Kyl, who belonged to the Republican Party, became a senator in the year 2001. Which state did he represent?
Arizona

941. In the year 1998, whom did Buddy MacKay succeed as the Governor of Florida?
Lawton Chiles

942. Name any one award Arnold Schwarzenegger received in the year 1977.
Golden Globe Award for New Star of the Year – Actor

943. Jim DeMint became a US senator from South Carolina in the year 2011. Where was he born?
Greenville

944. David Vitter became a senator in the year 2011. Which state did he represent?
Louisiana

945. Name any one award Josephine Roche received in the year 1986.
Colorado Women's Hall of Fame

946. Whom did Jerry Brown marry in the year 2005?

Anne Gust

947. In which year did Richard Riley become the Governor of South Carolina?
1979

948. Can you name the politician who received the «Moses-Mendelssohn-Preis» award in the year 1986?
Yehudi Menuhin

949. What medal did Jesse Jackson receive in the year 1989?
Spingarn Medal

950. In the year 1982, whom did Chuck Robb succeed as the Governor of Virginia?
John N. Dalton

951. Can you name the politician who received the «National Humanities Medal» in the year 2012?
Edward L. Ayers

952. From which university did Giorgos Kaminis get his master's degree in jurisprudence?
Panthéon-Assas University

953. Can you name the politician who received the «Hans von Bülow Medal» in the year 1979?
Yehudi Menuhin

954. What is the name of Elizabeth Cheney's father?
Dick Cheney

955. John F. Reed became a senator in the year 2017. Which state did he represent?
Rhode Island

956. Name any one award George John Mitchell Jr. received in the year 1998.
Félix Houphouët-Boigny Peace Prize

957. In the year 1999, whom did Gray Davis succeed as the Governor of California?
Pete Wilson

958. Bob Kerrey became a US senator from Nebraska in the year 1995. Where was he born?
Lincoln

959. What is the name of Peter W. Galbraith's father?
John Kenneth Galbraith

960. In the year 1998, whom did Nancy Hollister succeed as the Governor of Ohio?
George Voinovich

961. Who replaced Dean Heller as the senator from Nevada in the year 2011?
Jacky Rosen

962. Can you name the politician who received the «Humanist of the Year» award in the year 1985?
John Kenneth Galbraith

963. Ed Markey became a senator in the year 2013. Which state did he represent?
Massachusetts

964. Can you name the politician who received the «Person of the Year, American Chamber of Commerce in Japan» award in the year 2016?
Caroline Kennedy

965. Byron Dorgan, who belonged to the Democratic

Party, became a senator in the year 2009. Which state did he represent?
North Dakota

966. Who replaced Jeff Sessions as the senator from Alabama in the year 1997?
Luther Strange

967. Chris Murphy, who belonged to the Democratic Party, became a senator in the year 2017. Which state did he represent?
Connecticut

968. Can you name the politician who received the «Pugsley Medal» in the year 1942?
Harold L. Ickes

969. Who became the mayor of Frederick in the year 2002?
Jennifer Dougherty

970. Jim Mountain Inhofe became a senator in the year 2009. Which state did he represent?
Oklahoma

971. Name any one award Joycelyn Elders received in the year 1991.
Candace Award

972. Jim Jeffords became a US senator from Vermont in the year 1995. Where was he born?
Rutland

973. What is the name of Mike Pence's mother?
Nancy Jane Pence

974. Patty Murray became a US senator from Washington

in the year 2013. Where was she born?
Seattle

975. Where was Bill Nelson, a senator from Florida, born?
Miami

976. In which year did Frank D. White become the Governor of Arkansas?
1981

977. Richard Shelby, who belonged to the Republican Party, became a senator in the year 2003. Which state did he represent?
Alabama

978. In the year 1995, whom did George W. Bush succeed as the Governor of Texas?
Ann Richards

979. Name any one award Newt Gingrich received in the year 1995.
Time Person of the Year

980. Can you name the politician who received the «Humboldt Prize» in the year 1995?
Steven Chu

981. In which year did Dave Heineman become the Governor of Nebraska?
2005

982. Can you name the politician who received the «Spingarn Medal» in the year 1963?
Medgar Evers

983. Dan Coats became a US senator from Indiana in the year 2015. Where was he born?

Jackson

984. Whom did Rand Paul marry in the year 1990?
Kelley Paul

985. Name any one award Franklin Delano Roosevelt received in the year 1948.
Knight Grand Cross of the Military Order of William

986. Tammy Duckworth became a senator in the year 2017. Which state did she represent?
Illinois

987. Can you name the politician who received the «National Women's Hall of Fame» award in the year 1990?
Barbara Jordan

988. What medal did Mary Ann Glendon receive in the year 2005?
National Humanities Medal

989. Don Nickles became a senator in the year 2003. Which state did he represent?
Oklahoma

990. Mike DeWine became a senator in the year 2003. Which state did he represent?
Ohio

991. Where did Mark Takano work as the president in the year 1992?
Riverside Community College District

992. Lisa Murkowski became a senator in the year 2007. Which state did she represent?
Alaska

993. Amy Klobuchar, who belonged to the Democratic Party, became a senator in the year 2015. Which state did she represent?
Minnesota

994. Where did Elihu Harris work as a chancellor in the year 2003?
Peralta Community College District

995. In which year did Sarah Palin marry Todd Palin?
1988

996. What is the name of Jeb Bush's father?
George H. W. Bush

997. Can you name the politician who received the «Ernst Reuter Medal» in the year 1962?
Robert F. Kennedy

998. Harry Reid became a US senator from Nevada in the year 1993. Where was he born?
Searchlight

999. Can you name the politician who received the «Lenin Peace Prize» in the year 1979?
Angela Davis

1000. Don Nickles became a US senator from Oklahoma in the year 1999. Where was he born?
Ponca City

1001. Ron Lee Wyden became a senator in the year 1999. Which state did he represent?
Oregon

1002. Name any one award Steven Chu received in the year 1990.

1003. Who had hired Mark Critz as an employee in the year 1998?
John Murtha

1004. Where was Connie Mack III, a Republican senator from Florida, born?
Philadelphia

1005. Name any one award Glenn Beck received in the year 2009.
Doublespeak Award

1006. In which year did Bill Owens become the Governor of Colorado?
1999

1007. In the year 1987, whom did Wallace G. Wilkinson succeed as the Governor of Kentucky?
Martha Layne Collins

1008. Name any one award Elizabeth Dole received in the year 1995.
Raoul Wallenberg Award

1009. Who had hired Dana Rohrabacher as a press secretary in the year 1976?
Ronald Reagan

1010. Name any one award Jimmie Davis received in the year 1998.
Grammy Hall of Fame

1011. Jeff Bingaman became a US senator from New Mexico in the year 2005. Where was he born?
El Paso

1012. Can you name the politician who received the «National Book Award for Young People's Literature» in the year 2016?
John Lewis

1013. Name any one award Sam Nunn received in the year 2004.
Heinz Award

1014. Whom did Elizabeth Dole marry in the year 1975?
Bob Dole

1015. Can you name the politician who received the «Time Person of the Year» award in the year 2016?
Donald Trump

1016. Who had hired Dana Rohrabacher as a speechwriter in the year 1981?
Ronald Reagan

1017. What medal did Ben Carson get in the year 2006?
Spingarn Medal

1018. What is the name of Elizabeth Cheney's mother?
Lynne Cheney

1019. Name any one award John Kenneth Galbraith received in the year 2000.
Leontief Prize for Advancing the Frontiers of Economic Thought

1020. Name any one award Wendell H. Ford received in the year 1993.
James Madison Award

1021. Where was Ben Nelson, a Democratic senator from

Nebraska, born?
McCook

1022. Name any one award John R. Gregg received in the year 2002.
Sagamore of the Wabash

1023. In the year 1991, whom did Pete Wilson succeed as the Governor of California?
George Deukmejian

1024. Can you name the politician who received the «Lasker-Bloomberg Public Service Award» in the year 1988?
Lowell P. Weicker

1025. In which year did Edward Mezvinsky marry Marjorie Margolies-Mezvinsky?
1975

1026. Where was Max Baucus, a Democratic senator from Montana, born?
Helena

1027. Can you name the politician who received the «Mount Holyoke College Mary Lyon Award» in the year 1984?
Elaine Chao

1028. Patty Murray, who belonged to the Democratic Party, became a senator in the year 2003. Which state did she represent?
Washington

1029. In the year 1999, whom did Tom Vilsack succeed as the Governor of Iowa?
Terry Branstad

1030. Can you name the politician who received the «AAAS Philip Hauge Abelson Prize» in the year 2010?
Rush D. Holt, Jr.

1031. Whom did Hillary Clinton replace as the senator from New York in the year 2001?
Daniel Patrick Moynihan

1032. Where did Noreen Evans get her Juris Doctor degree in law from?
University of the Pacific

1033. In which year did Dick Celeste become the Governor of Ohio?
1983

1034. Name any one award John Cornyn received in the year 2015.
James Madison Award

1035. Dick Durbin, who belonged to the Democratic Party, became a senator in the year 2007. Which state did he represent?
Illinois

1036. In the year 1973, whom did James Holshouser succeed as the Governor of North Carolina?
Robert W. Scott

1037. In which year did Jim Gilmore become the Governor of Virginia?
1998

1038. In which year did Mitt Romney marry Ann Romney?
1969

1039. Patrick Leahy became a US senator from Vermont in the year 2013. Where was he born?
Montpelier

1040. In the year 1993, whom did Tom Carper succeed as the Governor of Delaware?
Dale E. Wolf

1041. Where was Max Cleland, a Democratic senator from Georgia, born?
Atlanta

1042. Can you name the politician who received the «European of the Year» award in the year 2006?
Ayaan Hirsi Ali

1043. Harry Reid, who belonged to the Democratic Party, became a senator in the year 2015. Which state did he represent?
Nevada

1044. Can you name the politician who received the «California Hall of Fame» award in the year 2007?
Earl Warren

1045. Evan Bayh, who belonged to the Democratic Party, became a senator in the year 2005. Which state did he represent?
Indiana

1046. Can you name the politician who received the «Alston-Jones International Civil and Human Rights Award» in the year 2010?
Julian Bond

1047. Where was Patrick Joseph Toomey, a Republican senator from Pennsylvania, born?

Providence

1048. What medal did Sandra Day O'Connor receive in the year 2009?
Presidential Medal of Freedom

1049. In the year 2003, whom did Ernie Fletcher succeed as the Governor of Kentucky?
Paul E. Patton

1050. Name any one award George H. W. Bush received in the year 2002.
Eric-M.-Warburg-Award

1051. Whom did Paul S. Trible, Jr. replace as the senator from Virginia in the year 1983?
Harry F. Byrd, Jr.

1052. Where was Mike Crapo, a Republican senator from Idaho, born?
Bonneville County

1053. In which year did Rick Scott become the Governor of Florida?
2011

1054. What is the name of John V. Tunney's mother?
Polly Lauder Tunney

1055. What is the name of Richard M. Daley's father?
Richard J. Daley

1056. Can you name the politician who received the «Grand Cross of the Order of the Southern Cross» award in the year 1946?
Dwight D. Eisenhower

1057. Name any one award Dixy Lee Ray received in the year 1975.
William Procter Prize for Scientific Achievement

1058. John F. Reed, who belonged to the Democratic Party, became a senator in the year 2011. Which state did he represent?
Rhode Island

1059. In the year 2001, whom did Ruth Ann Minner succeed as the Governor of Delaware?
Tom Carper

1060. Pat Roberts became a senator in the year 2007. Which state did he represent?
Kansas

1061. What medal did Robert McNamara receive in the year 1983?
Medal of honor Dag Hammarskjold

1062. Who had hired Rodney L. Davis as a member of congressional staff in the year 1997?
John Shimkus

1063. Where was Dan Coats, a Republican senator from Indiana, born?
Jackson

1064. Where was Patrick Leahy, a Democratic senator from Vermont, born?
Montpelier

1065. What is the name of Edward M. Kennedy, Jr.'s father?
Ted Kennedy

1066. Can you name the politician who received the «Doublespeak Award» in the year 1988?
Frank Carlucci

1067. Johnny Isakson became a senator in the year 2011. Which state did he represent?
Georgia

1068. Can you name the politician who received the «MTV Movie Award for Best Male Performance» in the year 1992?
Arnold Schwarzenegger

1069. Can you name the politician who received the «Hoover Medal» in the year 1960?
Dwight D. Eisenhower

1070. In the year 1971, whom did Richard F. Kneip succeed as the Governor of South Dakota?
Frank Farrar

1071. In the year 1995, whom did Gary Johnson succeed as the Governor of New Mexico?
Bruce King

1072. Whom did Laura Bush marry in the year 1977?
George W. Bush

1073. In the year 1985, whom did James G. Martin succeed as the Governor of North Carolina?
Jim Hunt

1074. Can you name the politician who received the «Light of Truth Award» in the year 2005?
Lowell Thomas Jr.

1075. What is the name of Tulsi Gabbard's father?

Mike Gabbard

1076. Craig L. Thomas became a US senator from Wyoming in the year 2001. Where was he born?
Cody

1077. Name any one award John Kerry received in the year 2016.
Grand Cross 1st class of the Order of Merit of the Federal Republic of Germany

1078. Can you name the politician who received the «National Humanities Medal» in the year 2001?
José Cisneros

1079. Can you name the politician who received the «Presidential Medal of Freedom» in the year 2017?
Joe Biden

1080. Name any one award Claiborne Pell received in the year 1997.
Light of Truth Award

1081. Who replaced Max Cleland as the senator from Georgia in the year 1997?
Saxby Chambliss

1082. Who replaced Dean Barkley as the senator from Minnesota in the year 2002?
Norm Coleman

1083. Name any one award Jesse White received in the year 1999.
Chicago Gay and Lesbian Hall of Fame

1084. Name any one award Sharon Pratt Kelly received in the year 1991.

Candace Award

1085. Name any one award Helen Berg received in the year 1976.
Star of People's Friendship

1086. Can you name the politician who received the «honorary doctor of the Yale University» award in the year 2010?
Steven Chu

1087. Can you name the politician who received the «Chicago Gay and Lesbian Hall of Fame» award in the year 1996?
Greg Harris

1088. Can you name the politician who received the «Lasker-Bloomberg Public Service Award» in the year 1978?
Elliot Richardson

1089. Can you name the politician who received the «Congressional Gold Medal» in the year 2000?
Nancy Reagan

1090. Name any one award William Perry received in the year 2016.
California Hall of Fame

1091. Who had hired Phil Hare as an employee in the year 1983?
Lane Evans

1092. Can you name the politician who received the «Adolph Lomb Medal» in the year 1958?
Edward L. O'Neill

1093. Can you name the politician who received the «Presidential Medal of Freedom» in the year 2011?
John Lewis

1094. Can you name the politician who received the «Knight Grand Cross of the Order of Merit of the Italian Republic» award in the year 1987?
Rita Levi-Montalcini

1095. Can you name the politician who received the «Rachel Carson Award» in the year 2013?
Lady Bird Johnson

1096. Paul Coverdell became a senator in the year 1993. Which state did he represent?
Georgia

1097. J. Bennett Johnston, Jr. became a senator in the year 1991. Which state did he represent?
Louisiana

1098. Trent Lott became a US senator from Mississippi in the year 2005. Where was he born?
Grenada

1099. Where did Jeb Bush get his Bachelor of Arts degree in Latin American studies from?
University of Texas at Austin

1100. Name any one award Michael Bloomberg received in the year 2014.
honorary doctor of Harvard University

1101. Can you name the politician who received the «Candace Award» in the year 1984?
Constance Baker Motley

1102. In the year 2000, whom did Rick Perry succeed as the Governor of Texas?
George W. Bush

1103. Name any one award Henry Martin Jackson received in the year 1969.
Sierra Club John Muir Award

1104. Joe Lieberman, who belonged to the Democratic Party, became a senator in the year 1991. Which state did he represent?
Connecticut

1105. Name any one award Antonia Novello received in the year 2004.
Hispanic Scientist of the Year Award

1106. Can you name the politician who received the «ASCB Public Service Award» in the year 2007?
Michael Castle

1107. Name any one award John Podesta received in the year 2015.
Ansel Adams Award

1108. Name any one award Ronald Noble received in the year 2011.
Hilal-e-Pakistan

1109. Can you name the politician who received the «Spingarn Medal» in the year 2002?
John Lewis

1110. In the year 1985, whom did Edward D. DiPrete succeed as the Governor of Rhode Island?
J. Joseph Garrahy

1111. Bob Packwood became a US senator from Oregon in the year 1969. Where was he born?
Portland

1112. Name any one award Elizabeth Dole received in the year 1994.
Maxwell Finland Award

1113. Can you name the politician who received the «Reebok Human Rights Award» in the year 1988?
Winona LaDuke

1114. In which year did Jon Corzine become the Governor of New Jersey?
2006

1115. Can you name the politician who received the «Col. Arthur T. Marix Congressional Leadership Award» in the year 2014?
Bernie Sanders

1116. Rick Santorum, who belonged to the Republican Party, became a senator in the year 1999. Which state did he represent?
Pennsylvania

1117. Name any one award Jennifer Granholm received in the year 2004.
Michigan Women's Hall of Fame

1118. Conrad Burns became a US senator from Montana in the year 2005. Where was he born?
Gallatin

1119. What is the name of David René de Rothschild's mother?
Alix Freiin Schey von Koromla

1120. In the year 2019, Kylie Oversen worked as the party chair in which political party?
North Dakota Democratic-Nonpartisan League Party

1121. Where was Al D'Amato, a Republican senator from New York, born?
Brooklyn

1122. Name any one award Richard M. Daley received in the year 2008.
Chandler Robbins Award

1123. Name any one award Janet Yellen received in the year 1998.
honorary degree

1124. Where was John McCain, a Republican senator from Arizona, born?
Coco Solo

1125. John F. Reed, who belonged to the Democratic Party, became a senator in the year 2015. Which state did he represent?
Rhode Island

1126. In which year did Nancy Lange marry Pedro Pablo Kuczynski?
1997

1127. In which year did Jim Gibbons become the Governor of Nevada?
2007

1128. Whom did Steven Mnuchin marry in the year 1999?
Heather deForest Crosby

1129. Whom did Donald Trump marry in the year 1977?
Ivana Trump

1130. Can you name the politician who received the «Hoover Medal» in the year 2001?
Richard H. Stanley

1131. Fred Thompson, who belonged to the Republican Party, became a senator in the year 1997. Which state did he represent?
Tennessee

1132. Can you name the politician who received the «Leo-Baeck-Medal» in the year 2006?
James Wolfensohn

1133. In which year did Ronnie Musgrove become the Governor of Mississippi?
2000

1134. Paul Wellstone became a senator in the year 1991. Which state did he represent?
Minnesota

1135. Where did Dennis Daugaard get his Bachelor of Science degree in government from?
University of South Dakota

1136. In the year 1983, whom did Bill Clinton succeed as the Governor of Arkansas?
Frank D. White

1137. Where was Olympia Snowe, a senator from Maine, born?
Augusta

1138. In the year 1991, whom did Ben Nelson succeed as

the Governor of Nebraska?
Kay A. Orr

1139. Whom did Ann McLaughlin Korologos marry in the year 1975?
John McLaughlin

1140. In the year 1982, whom did Pedro Tenorio succeed as the Governor of the Northern Mariana Islands?
Carlos S. Camacho

1141. Can you name the politician who received the «Theatre World Award» in the year 1960?
Patty Duke

1142. Who replaced John Edwards as the senator from North Carolina in the year 1999?
Richard M. Burr

1143. Can you name the politician who received the «Siena Medal» in the year 1988?
Anne M. Burke

1144. Can you name the politician who received the «Ewald von Kleist award» in the year 2009?
Henry Kissinger

1145. Can you name the politician who received the «Genesis Prize» in the year 2014?
Michael Bloomberg

1146. Where did Sean Spicer get his master's degree in strategic studies from?
Naval War College

1147. Where was William Cohen, a Republican senator from Maine, born?

Bangor

1148. George John Mitchell Jr. became a US senator from Maine in the year 1980. Where was he born?
Waterville

1149. What is the name of Al Gore's father?
Albert Arnold Gore

1150. What is the name of Mark Shriver's father?
Sargent Shriver

1151. Name any one award Rita Levi-Montalcini received in the year 2008.
Grand Officer of the Legion of Honour

1152. Where was Jon Kyl, a Republican senator from Arizona, born?
Oakland

1153. Can you name the politician who received the «Presidential Medal of Freedom» in the year 1996?
James Brady

1154. Can you name the politician who received the «honorary citizen of Magdeburg» award in the year 1972?
Angela Davis

1155. Who became the mayor of South Bend in the year 2012?
Pete Buttigieg

1156. Frank Murkowski became a senator in the year 1991. Which state did he represent?
Alaska

1157. Kay Bailey Hutchison, who belonged to the

Republican Party, became a senator in the year 1999. Which state did she represent?
Texas

1158. Who replaced Byron Dorgan as the senator from North Dakota in the year 1992?
John Hoeven

1159. What is the name of Elaine Chao's father?
James S.C. Chao

1160. Can you name the politician who received the «Doctor of Law (honorary)» award in the year 2001?
Madeleine Albright

1161. Joe Lieberman became a US senator from Connecticut in the year 2003. Where was he born?
Stamford

1162. Whom did Elizabeth Warren marry in the year 1968?
Jim Warren

1163. Name any one award Bob Dole received in the year 1998.
Theodore Roosevelt Award

1164. Name any one award Cindy Sheehan received in the year 2007.
Thomas Merton Award

1165. Name any one award Janet Yellen received in the year 2012.
50 Most Influential

1166. Who had hired Doris Matsui as a helper in the year 1993?
Bill Clinton

1167. What is the name of Lincoln Chafee's mother?
Virginia Chafee

1168. In the year 1996, Jerry Moran was a member of which organization?
Kansas Chamber of Commerce

1169. Where was Dirk Kempthorne, a Republican senator from Idaho, born?
San Diego

1170. In which year did Lawrence Summers marry Elisa New?
2005

1171. Who became the mayor of Jackson in the year 2013?
Chokwe Lumumba

1172. Kent Conrad became a US senator from North Dakota in the year 1997. Where was he born?
Bismarck

1173. Name any one award Mary Carey received in the year 2013.
AVN Hall of Fame

1174. Name any one award Rudy Giuliani received in the year 2018.
Doublespeak Award

1175. What medal did Yehudi Menuhin get in the year 1997?
Otto Hahn Peace Medal

1176. Can you name the politician who received the

«Lasker-Bloomberg Public Service Award» in the year 2005?
Nancy Brinker

1177. In which year did George W. Bush marry Laura Bush?
1977

1178. Michael Bennet became a US senator from Colorado in the year 2011. Where was he born?
New Delhi

1179. Where was Sheldon Whitehouse, a Democratic senator from Rhode Island, born?
Manhattan

1180. Hillary Clinton, who belonged to the Democratic Party, became a senator in the year 2007. Which state did she represent?
New York

1181. Where was Bob Graham, a Democratic senator from Florida, born?
Coral Gables

1182. In which year did Dianne Feinstein marry Richard C. Blum?
1980

1183. Who became the mayor of Union City in the year 1986?
Robert Menendez

1184. In the year 2000, George LeMieux worked as a chairperson in which political party?
Republican Party

1185. Where was Paul Wellstone, a Democratic senator from Minnesota, born?
Washington, D.C.

1186. Tom Carper became a US senator from Delaware in the year 2005. Where was he born?
Beckley

1187. What medal did Henry D. Lindsley get in the year 1919?
Distinguished Service Medal

1188. In which year did Tom Hayden marry Jane Fonda?
1973

1189. Name any one award Paul Nitze received in the year 1990.
Eric-M.-Warburg-Award

1190. Whom did Chuck Robb replace as the senator from Virginia in the year 1989?
Paul S. Trible, Jr.

1191. Mark Warner became a US senator from Virginia in the year 2015. Where was he born?
Indianapolis

1192. Where did Kristina Keneally get her Master of Arts degree in religious studies from?
Marquette University

1193. Dean Heller became a US senator from Nevada in the year 2013. Where was he born?
Castro Valley

1194. Name any one award Jimmy Carter received in the year 1998.

1195. Gary Peters became a US senator from Michigan in the year 2017. Where was he born?
Pontiac

1196. What is the name of Joseph P. Kennedy II's father?
Robert F. Kennedy

1197. From which university did Elizabeth Warren get her Bachelor of Science degree in audiology?
University of Houston

1198. In the year 1975, whom did Jerry Apodaca succeed as the Governor of New Mexico?
Bruce King

1199. Whom did Peter T. Snowe marry in the year 1969?
Olympia Snowe

1200. Where did Mikie Sherrill get her Master of Science degree in economic history from?
London School of Economics

1201. Who replaced Jon Kyl as the senator from Arizona in the year 1995?
Jeff Flake

1202. Name any one award Ralph Nader received in the year 2017.
Gandhi Peace Award

1203. Name any one award John F. Kennedy received in the year 1951.
Grand Officer of the Order of the Star of Italian Solidarity

1204. Mark Dayton became a US senator from Minnesota

in the year 2001. Where was he born?
Minneapolis

1205. Mary Landrieu, who belonged to the Democratic Party, became a senator in the year 2013. Which state did she represent?
Louisiana

1206. Jeff Merkley became a senator in the year 2015. Which state did he represent?
Oregon

1207. Can you name the politician who received the «Labor Hall of Honor» award in the year 1999?
Terence V. Powderly

1208. Robert Jones Portman became a senator in the year 2017. Which state did he represent?
Ohio

1209. Name any one award Joel Anderson received in the year 2016.
EFF Pioneer Award

1210. In the year 2003, whom did Janet Napolitano succeed as the Governor of Arizona?
Jane Dee Hull

1211. What medal did J. Edgar Hoover receive in the year 1939?
Public Welfare Medal

1212. Larry Pressler became a US senator from South Dakota in the year 1991. Where was he born?
Humboldt

1213. In which year did Steven Mnuchin marry Louise

Linton?
2017

1214. Name any one award Ramona Martinez received in the year 2010.
Colorado Women's Hall of Fame

1215. In which year did Arne Carlson become the Governor of Minnesota?
1991

1216. Where was Orrin Hatch, a Republican senator from Utah, born?
Homestead Park

1217. Can you name the politician who received the «National Defense Service Medal» in the year 1953?
Dwight D. Eisenhower

1218. Russ Feingold became a senator in the year 2003. Which state did he represent?
Wisconsin

1219. In the year 2007, whom did Eliot Spitzer succeed as the Governor of New York?
George Pataki

1220. Where was Bill Bradley, a senator from New Jersey, born?
Crystal City

1221. Can you name the politician who received the «honorary doctor of the Hebrew University of Jerusalem» award in the year 1976?
Daniel Patrick Moynihan

1222. Chris Coons became a senator in the year 2017.

Which state did he represent?
Delaware

1223. Can you name the politician who received the «Doublespeak Award» in the year 2005?
Philip Cooney

1224. Jim Mountain Inhofe, who belonged to the Republican Party, became a senator in the year 2005. Which state did he represent?
Oklahoma

1225. Can you name the politician who received the «Bancroft Prize» in the year 1957?
George F. Kennan

1226. Whom did Chaka Fattah marry in the year 2001?
Renee Chenault-Fattah

1227. Name any one award Kathleen N. Straus received in the year 2000.
Michigan Women's Hall of Fame

1228. Where was Orrin Hatch, a senator from Utah, born?
Homestead Park

1229. Name any one award Ramsey Clark received in the year 2008.
United Nations Prize in the Field of Human Rights

1230. James Lankford became a senator in the year 2017. Which state did he represent?
Oklahoma

1231. Name any one award Dwight D. Eisenhower received in the year 1943.
Africa Star

1232. In which year did Sonny Bono marry Susie Coelho?
1981

1233. Can you name the politician who received the «James Madison Award» in the year 2008?
Russ Feingold

1234. Can you name the politician who received the «Audubon Medal» in the year 1977?
Russell W. Peterson

1235. Chris Dodd became a US senator from Connecticut in the year 1997. Where was he born?
Willimantic

1236. Where did Ronnie Flippo get his Bachelor of Science degree in accounting from?
University of North Alabama

1237. Bill Nelson, who belonged to the Democratic Party, became a senator in the year 2003. Which state did he represent?
Florida

1238. What medal did Gaylord Nelson receive in the year 1995?
Presidential Medal of Freedom

1239. Name any one award Ben Bernanke received in the year 2014.
Adam Smith Award

1240. In which year did Kenny Guinn become the Governor of Nevada?
1999

1241. Name any one award Eric Greitens received in the year 2005.
White House Fellows

1242. In the year 1978, whom did Harvey L. Wollman succeed as the Governor of South Dakota?
Richard F. Kneip

1243. Whom did Jim Webb marry in the year 1981?
Jo Ann Krukar

1244. What medal did David Price receive in the year 2002?
Wilbur Cross Medal

1245. Who became the mayor of Houston in the year 1982?
Kathryn J. Whitmire

1246. Who replaced Mary Landrieu as the senator from Louisiana in the year 1997?
Bill Cassidy

1247. Name any one award Tip O'Neill received in the year 1991.
Lasker-Bloomberg Public Service Award

1248. Chuck Grassley, who belonged to the Republican Party, became a senator in the year 2005. Which state did he represent?
Iowa

1249. In the year 1991, whom did Lowell P. Weicker succeed as the Governor of Connecticut?
William O'Neill

1250. Richard Shelby, who belonged to the Republican

Party, became a senator in the year 2013. Which state did he represent?
Alabama

1251. Who replaced Craig L. Thomas as the senator from Wyoming in the year 1995?
John Barrasso

1252. Name any one award Rita Levi-Montalcini received in the year 1986.
Commander of the Order of Merit of the Italian Republic

1253. From which university did Trip Pittman get his Bachelor of Science degree in commerce?
University of Alabama

1254. In which year did Jane Swift become the Governor of Massachusetts?
2001

1255. Saxby Chambliss became a senator in the year 2003. Which state did he represent?
Georgia

1256. Who replaced Gordon J. Humphrey as the senator from New Hampshire in the year 1979?
Robert C. Smith

1257. Tim Scott, who belonged to the Republican Party, became a senator in the year 2015. Which state did he represent?
South Carolina

1258. Wayne Allard, who belonged to the Republican Party, became a senator in the year 2005. Which state did he represent?
Colorado

1259. Name any one award Martha Griffiths received in the year 1993.
National Women's Hall of Fame

1260. What is the name of John McCain's mother?
Roberta McCain

1261. What is the name of John Kerry's mother?
Rosemary Forbes Kerry

1262. Name any one award Herbert A. Simon received in the year 1989.
William James Fellow Award

1263. Can you name the politician who received the «Doublespeak Award» in the year 2016?
Donald Trump

1264. From which university did Mo Brooks get his Bachelor of Arts degree in economics?
Duke University

1265. Whom did Mark Pryor replace as the senator from Arkansas in the year 2003?
Tim Hutchinson

1266. Where did Kristina Keneally get her Bachelor of Arts degree in political science from?
University of Dayton

1267. Can you name the politician who received the «National Medal of Science» in the year 1987?
Rita Levi-Montalcini

1268. Can you name the politician who received the «Profile in Courage Award» in the year 1999?

John McCain

1269. What medal did John Kenneth Galbraith receive in the year 1993?
Lomonosov Gold Medal

1270. In the year 1985, whom did Michael Castle succeed as the Governor of Delaware?
Pierre Samuel du Pont IV

1271. Name any one award Jacqueline Cochran received in the year 1993.
National Women's Hall of Fame

1272. Name any one award Condoleezza Rice received in the year 2010.
Horatio Alger Award

1273. John F. Reed, who belonged to the Democratic Party, became a senator in the year 1997. Which state did he represent?
Rhode Island

1274. Where did Gary Peters get his Master of Arts degree in philosophy from?
Michigan State University

1275. Can you name the politician who received the «Time Person of the Year» award in the year 2012?
Barack Obama

1276. Can you name the politician who received the «doctor honoris causa» award in the year 2009?
Hillary Clinton

1277. Bernie Sanders became a US senator from Vermont in the year 2009. Where was he born?

Brooklyn

1278. Whom did Jim Webb marry in the year 1968?
Barbara Samorajczyk

1279. Can you name the politician who received the «honorary doctor of the McGill University» award in the year 2009?
Bill Clinton

1280. Can you name the politician who received the «Goethe Plaque of the City of Frankfurt» award in the year 1952?
John J. McCloy

1281. Where was Jerry Moran, a Republican senator from Kansas, born?
Great Bend

1282. Mike Enzi became a US senator from Wyoming in the year 2001. Where was he born?
Bremerton

1283. Name any one award Ed Asner received in the year 1982.
Paul Robeson Award

1284. Who wrote the book «Immigration Wars: Forging an American Solution»?
Jeb Bush

1285. Can you name the politician who received the «Spingarn Medal» in the year 1936?
John Hope

1286. Name any one award Herbert A. Simon received in the year 1969.

1287. Rand Paul, who belonged to the Republican Party, became a senator in the year 2011. Which state did he represent?
Kentucky

1288. Michael Bennet became a US senator from Colorado in the year 2013. Where was he born?
New Delhi

1289. Name any one award Rita Levi-Montalcini received in the year 1981.
Rosenstiel Award

1290. Can you name the politician who received the «Public Welfare Medal» in the year 2014?
John Porter

1291. Can you name the politician who received the «Audubon Medal» in the year 1994?
Jimmy Carter

1292. Can you name the politician who received the «Honorary doctor of the Free University of Berlin» award in the year 1953?
Lucius D. Clay

1293. Paul Sarbanes became a senator in the year 1995. Which state did he represent?
Maryland

1294. Can you name the politician who received the «Knight Grand Cross of the Order of Merit of the Italian Republic» award in the year 2007?
Nancy Pelosi

1295. Can you name the politician who received the «honorary doctorate of the University of Valencia» award in the year 1999?
Yehudi Menuhin

1296. Can you name the politician who received the «IEEE Medal of Honor» in the year 1982?
John Tukey

1297. Steve Daines, who belonged to the Republican Party, became a senator in the year 2017. Which state did he represent?
Montana

1298. Evan Bayh, who belonged to the Democratic Party, became a senator in the year 2009. Which state did he represent?
Indiana

1299. In the year 1975, whom did Jerry Brown succeed as the Governor of California?
Ronald Reagan

1300. Can you name the politician who received the «Public Welfare Medal» in the year 1982?
Paul Rogers

1301. Can you name the politician who received the «Peace Prize of the German Book Trade» in the year 1979?
Yehudi Menuhin

1302. Name any one award Ronald Reagan received in the year 1983.
Doublespeak Award

1303. Jeff Sessions became a US senator from Alabama in the year 2001. Where was he born?
Selma

1304. Bill Frist became a US senator from Tennessee in the year 2005. Where was he born?
Nashville

1305. Gordon H. Smith became a senator in the year 2003. Which state did he represent?
Oregon

1306. In the year 2005, whom did Brian Schweitzer succeed as the Governor of Montana?
Judy Martz

1307. In which year did Olympia Snowe marry John R. McKernan?
1989

1308. In the year 1995, whom did David Beasley succeed as the Governor of South Carolina?
Carroll A. Campbell, Jr.

1309. Name any one award Tom Foley received in the year 2000.
Person of the Year, American Chamber of Commerce in Japan

1310. Who had hired Hilda Solis as United States Cabinet in the year 2009?
Barack Obama

1311. In the year 2005, whom did Joe Manchin succeed as the Governor of West Virginia?
Bob Wise

1312. Can you name the politician who received the «Fulbright Prize» in the year 1994?
Jimmy Carter

1313. Whom did Elizabeth Warren marry in the year 1980?
Bruce Mann

1314. Name any one award Larry McKeon received in the year 1997.
Chicago Gay and Lesbian Hall of Fame

1315. Can you name the politician who received the «G. K. Gilbert Award» in the year 1989?
Harrison Schmitt

1316. Where did Hank Brown get his Master of Laws degree in tax law from?
George Washington University

1317. From which university did Ilhan Omar get her bachelor's degree in political science?
North Dakota State University

1318. What is the name of Tulsi Gabbard's mother?
Carol Porter Gabbard

1319. In the year 2008, whom did David Paterson succeed as the Governor of New York?
Eliot Spitzer

1320. In which year did Ben Cayetano become the Governor of Hawaii?
1994

1321. In which year did Benigno Fitial become the Governor of the Northern Mariana Islands?
2006

1322. In which year did Deval Patrick become the Governor of Massachusetts?
2007

1323. In the year 2013, whom did Eloy Inos succeed as the Governor of the Northern Mariana Islands?
Benigno Fitial

1324. Connie Mack III became a senator in the year 1989. Which state did he represent?
Florida

1325. Can you name the politician who received the «Champions of the Earth» award in the year 2007?
Al Gore

1326. Where did Kurt A. Vialet get his Bachelor of Arts degree in mathematics from?
University of the Virgin Islands

1327. Name any one award Madeleine Albright received in the year 1997.
Order of the White Lion

1328. Can you name the politician who received the «National Women's Hall of Fame» award in the year 1995?
Maggie Kuhn

1329. Who became the mayor of Tulsa in the year 1978?
Jim Mountain Inhofe

1330. Joe Donnelly became a US senator from Indiana in the year 2013. Where was he born?
Queens

1331. Name any one award Sam Nunn received in the year

2008.
Rumford Prize

1332. In the year 1995, whom did Bill Janklow succeed as the Governor of South Dakota?
Walter Dale Miller

1333. Where was Jeff Merkley, a Democratic senator from Oregon, born?
Myrtle Creek

1334. Can you name the politician who received the «Michigan Women's Hall of Fame» award in the year 1998?
Ruth Thompson

1335. Herb Kohl, who belonged to the Democratic Party, became a senator in the year 2011. Which state did he represent?
Wisconsin

1336. Can you name the politician who received the «Albert Schweitzer Prize for Humanitarianism» in the year 1987?
Jimmy Carter

1337. Mike Johanns, who belonged to the Republican Party, became a senator in the year 2011. Which state did he represent?
Nebraska

1338. What is the name of Shelley Moore Capito's mother?
Shelley Riley Moore

1339. Can you name the politician who received the «Spingarn Medal» in the year 1978?

1340. Hank Brown, who belonged to the Republican Party, became a senator in the year 1995. Which state did he represent?
Colorado

1341. Joe Lieberman, who belonged to the Democratic Party, became a senator in the year 1997. Which state did he represent?
Connecticut

1342. Where was Jim Bunning, a Republican senator from Kentucky, born?
Southgate

1343. Name any one award Janette Sadik-Khan received in the year 2012.
Rachel Carson Award

1344. Can you name the politician who received the «Benjamin Franklin Medal» in the year 2003?
Colin Powell

1345. Whom did Don Nickles replace as the senator from Oklahoma in the year 1981?
Henry Bellmon

1346. Where did Lori Lightfoot get her Bachelor of Arts degree in political science from?
University of Michigan

1347. Russ Feingold became a senator in the year 1999. Which state did he represent?
Wisconsin

1348. Where was Tom Daschle, a Democratic senator

from South Dakota, born?
Aberdeen

1349. In which year did Tipper Gore marry Al Gore?
1970

1350. Where was Doug Jones, a Democratic senator from Alabama, born?
Fairfield

1351. What medal did John F. Kennedy receive in the year 1943?
Navy and Marine Corps Medal

1352. John Boozman became a senator in the year 2017. Which state did he represent?
Arkansas

1353. Name any one award Paul Volcker received in the year 1987.
Francis Boyer Award

1354. Where was Kit Bond, a Republican senator from Missouri, born?
St. Louis

1355. What is the name of Barack Obama's father?
Barack Obama Sr.

1356. Ben Nighthorse Campbell became a senator in the year 1995. Which state did he represent?
Colorado

1357. Where was Mark Kirk, a Republican senator from Illinois, born?
Champaign

1358. What is the name of Margaret Hamburg's father?
David A. Hamburg

1359. In the year 2011, whom did Tom Corbett succeed as the Governor of Pennsylvania?
Ed Rendell

1360. In which year did Ivanka Trump marry Jared Kushner?
2009

1361. Name any one award John Grisham received in the year 2005.
Helmerich Award

1362. What medal did Hillary Clinton get in the year 2013?
Department of Defense Medal for Distinguished Public Service

1363. Name any one award Patricia Schroeder received in the year 1995.
National Women's Hall of Fame

1364. Where was Richard M. Burr, a Republican senator from North Carolina, born?
Charlottesville

1365. In which year did Jackie Chan marry Lin Feng-jiao?
1982

1366. Can you name the politician who received the «Francis Boyer Award» in the year 1993?
Dick Cheney

1367. Chris Murphy, who belonged to the Democratic Party, became a senator in the year 2015. Which state did he represent?
Connecticut

1368. Whom did Barack Obama marry in the year 1992?
Michelle Obama

1369. What medal did David K. E. Bruce get in the year 1971?
Benjamin Franklin Medal

1370. In the year 2006, Tammy Duckworth worked as a director in which government agency?
Illinois Department of Veterans Affairs

1371. From which university did Carina Vance Mafla get her master's degree in public health?
University of California, Berkeley

1372. Name any one award Sharpe James received in the year 1996.
New Jersey Mayors Hall of Fame

1373. Ben Nelson became a US senator from Nebraska in the year 2011. Where was he born?
McCook

1374. Name any one award Dave Bing received in the year 1977.
J. Walter Kennedy Citizenship Award

1375. In which year did Jack Dalrymple become the Governor of North Dakota?
2010

1376. In which year did Peter R. Orszag marry Bianna Golodryga?
2010

1377. Name any one award Stefan Heym received in the

year 1993.
Jerusalem Prize

1378. Where was Mark Dayton, a Democratic senator from Minnesota, born?
Minneapolis

1379. Peter Fitzgerald, who belonged to the Republican Party, became a senator in the year 2003. Which state did he represent?
Illinois

1380. Can you name the politician who received the «honorary doctor of Harvard University» award in the year 2009?
Steven Chu

1381. Name any one award Rahm Emanuel received in the year 2013.
Doublespeak Award

1382. Can you name the politician who received the «James Madison Award» in the year 2002?
John E. Moss

1383. Name any one award Angela Davis received in the year 1972.
Star of People's Friendship

1384. Can you name the politician who received the «National Women's Hall of Fame» award in the year 2011?
Donna Shalala

1385. Where was Richard Lugar, a Republican senator from Indiana, born?
Indianapolis

1386. Can you name the politician who received the «Officer of the Order of Australia» award in the year 1987?
James Wolfensohn

1387. Sam Brownback became a senator in the year 2001. Which state did he represent?
Kansas

1388. Bob P. Casey, Jr. became a senator in the year 2013. Which state did he represent?
Pennsylvania

1389. Name any one award Yehudi Menuhin received in the year 1968.
Jawaharlal Nehru Award for International Understanding

1390. In which year did Kirk Fordice become the Governor of Mississippi?
1992

1391. What medal did Henry Ford get in the year 1928?
Elliott Cresson Medal

1392. From which university did Mohamed Abdullahi Farmajo get his bachelor's degree in history?
University at Buffalo

1393. In the year 1986, whom did Steve Cowper succeed as the Governor of Alaska?
Bill Sheffield

1394. Where was Olympia Snowe, a Republican senator from Maine, born?
Augusta

1395. Kay Hagan became a US senator from North Carolina in the year 2013. Where was she born?

Shelby

1396. What is the name of Elaine Chao's mother?
Ruth Mulan Chu Chao

1397. Can you name the politician who received the «Colorado Women's Hall of Fame» award in the year 1985?
Mamie Eisenhower

1398. Pete Domenici became a senator in the year 2005. Which state did he represent?
New Mexico

1399. Harry Reid became a senator in the year 1997. Which state did he represent?
Nevada

1400. Whom did Michael Dukakis marry in the year 1963?
Kitty Dukakis

1401. In which year did Bob McDonnell become the Governor of Virginia?
2010

1402. In which year did Jim McGreevey marry Dina Matos?
2000

1403. Richard Lugar became a US senator from Indiana in the year 2007. Where was he born?
Indianapolis

1404. Robert Menendez, who belonged to the Democratic Party, became a senator in the year 2013. Which state did he represent?
New Jersey

1405. Pat Roberts became a US senator from Kansas in the year 2005. Where was he born?
Topeka

1406. Can you name the politician who received the «North Carolina Women's Hall of Fame» award in the year 2009?
Marie Colton

1407. Name any one award Dwight D. Eisenhower received in the year 1945.
Grand Cordon of the Order of Leopold

1408. Where did Mary Jo White get her master's degree in psychology from?
The New School

1409. Where was Jeff Bingaman, a Democratic senator from New Mexico, born?
El Paso

1410. Name any one award Nancy Brinker received in the year 2015.
National Women's Hall of Fame

1411. Can you name the politician who received the «Nansen Refugee Award» in the year 2009?
Ted Kennedy

1412. Who had hired Sean Spicer as White House Communications Director in the year 2017?
Donald Trump

1413. Jim Jeffords became a senator in the year 1997. Which state did he represent?
Vermont

1414. Kit Bond became a US senator from Missouri in the year 1993. Where was he born?
St. Louis

1415. Can you name the politician who received the «Ansel Adams Award» in the year 1982?
Jimmy Carter

1416. John Kerry became a senator in the year 1985. Which state did he represent?
Massachusetts

1417. Mike Enzi, who belonged to the Republican Party, became a senator in the year 2013. Which state did he represent?
Wyoming

1418. In which year did Tim Pawlenty become the Governor of Minnesota?
2003

1419. Name any one award Jeff Sessions received in the year 2014.
member of the Alabama Academy of Honor

1420. Can you name the politician who received the «Siena Medal» in the year 1996?
Nancy Brinker

1421. In which year did Jan Brewer become the Governor of Arizona?
2009

1422. Who replaced Bob Corker as the senator from Tennessee in the year 2007?
Marsha Blackburn

1423. Mazie Hirono, who belonged to the Democratic Party, became a senator in the year 2015. Which state did she represent?
Hawaii

1424. Name any one award Gaylord Nelson received in the year 2001.
Sierra Club John Muir Award

1425. Carl Levin became a senator in the year 1991. Which state did he represent?
Michigan

1426. Joni Ernst, who belonged to the Republican Party, became a senator in the year 2015. Which state did she represent?
Iowa

1427. Where did Robert A. Baines work as a chancellor in the year 2007?
Chester College of New England

1428. Can you name the politician who received the «Ripple of Hope Award» in the year 2014?
Hillary Clinton

1429. In which year did Anne Gorsuch Burford marry Robert F. Burford?
1983

1430. Can you name the politician who received the «Seán MacBride Peace Prize» in the year 2002?
Barbara Lee

1431. Where was Ben Nighthorse Campbell, a senator from Colorado, born?

Auburn

1432. Pete Domenici, who belonged to the Republican Party, became a senator in the year 1991. Which state did he represent?
New Mexico

1433. What is the name of Caroline Kennedy's father?
John F. Kennedy

1434. Can you name the politician who received the «FSF Award for the Advancement of Free Software» in the year 2002?
Lawrence Lessig

1435. Where did Emily Larson get her bachelor's degree in social work from?
The College of St. Scholastica

1436. Where was Mary Landrieu, a Democratic senator from Louisiana, born?
Arlington County

1437. In the year 1999, whom did Jesse Ventura succeed as the Governor of Minnesota?
Arne Carlson

1438. Herb Kohl became a US senator from Wisconsin in the year 1989. Where was he born?
Milwaukee

1439. In the year 1991, whom did George Voinovich succeed as the Governor of Ohio?
Dick Celeste

1440. Can you name the politician who received the «John Bates Clark Medal» in the year 1993?

1441. Ron Johnson became a US senator from Wisconsin in the year 2013. Where was he born?
Mankato

1442. Can you name the politician who received the «Michigan Women's Hall of Fame» award in the year 2005?
Debbie Stabenow

1443. What medal did Herbert Hoover receive in the year 1930?
Hoover Medal

1444. Can you name the politician who received the «honorary citizen of Shanghai» award in the year 2016?
Linda Tsao Yang

1445. Saxby Chambliss became a senator in the year 2011. Which state did he represent?
Georgia

1446. Can you name the politician who received the «Pardes Humanitarian Prize in Mental Health» in the year 2015?
Rosalynn Carter

1447. Can you name the politician who received the «Honorary doctorate of the University of South Carolina» award in the year 1923?
Ignacy Jan Paderewski

1448. In which year did Wilbur Ross marry Betsy McCaughey?
1995

1449. Kit Bond became a US senator from Missouri in the year 1999. Where was he born?
St. Louis

1450. Bernie Sanders, who belonged to the independent politician, became a senator in the year 2011. Which state did he represent?
Vermont

1451. Can you name the politician who received the «NBA All-Rookie Team» award in the year 1967?
Dave Bing

1452. Where was Blanche Lincoln, a Democratic senator from Arkansas, born?
Helena

1453. Can you name the politician who received the «Freedom Award» in the year 1970?
Jacob Koppel Javits

1454. Can you name the politician who received the «Edison Medal» in the year 1943?
Vannevar Bush

1455. What is the name of Michelle Obama's mother?
Marian Shields Robinson

1456. Gordon H. Smith, who belonged to the Republican Party, became a senator in the year 1999. Which state did he represent?
Oregon

1457. Bob Kerrey became a senator in the year 1993. Which state did he represent?
Nebraska

1458. Name any one award John Kenneth Galbraith received in the year 1972.
Honorary doctor of the Katholieke Universiteit Leuven

1459. Whom did Linda McMahon marry in the year 1966?
Vince McMahon

1460. Joe Lieberman became a senator in the year 2007. Which state did he represent?
Connecticut

1461. Sheila Frahm became a senator in the year 1996. Which state did she represent?
Kansas

1462. Can you name the politician who received the «Golden Horse Award for Best Leading Actor» in the year 1992?
Jackie Chan

1463. Trent Lott, who belonged to the Republican Party, became a senator in the year 1999. Which state did he represent?
Mississippi

1464. Name any one award Harvey Milk received in the year 2009.
California Hall of Fame

1465. Spencer Abraham became a senator in the year 1999. Which state did he represent?
Michigan

1466. In the year 1983, whom did Martha Layne Collins succeed as the Governor of Kentucky?
John Y. Brown

1467. What is the name of Michael Bennet's mother?
Susanne Klejman

1468. Can you name the politician who received the «Goldman Environmental Prize» in the year 2002?
Sarah James

1469. Chris Dodd became a senator in the year 2001. Which state did he represent?
Connecticut

1470. In which year did Tom Hayden marry Barbara Williams?
1993

1471. Can you name the politician who received the «James Watt International Medal» in the year 1939?
Henry Ford

1472. Whom did Richard Bryan replace as the senator from Nevada in the year 1989?
Chic Hecht

1473. What is the name of Albert II's mother?
Grace Kelly

1474. Jeff Bingaman became a US senator from New Mexico in the year 2009. Where was he born?
El Paso

1475. Where did Mitt Romney get his Juris Doctor degree in law from?
Harvard Law School

1476. What is the name of Ted Kennedy's mother?
Rose Kennedy

1477. Cory Booker, who belonged to the Democratic Party, became a senator in the year 2017. Which state did he represent?
New Jersey

1478. John Danforth became a senator in the year 1976. Which state did he represent?
Missouri

1479. Name any one award Ted Kennedy received in the year 2016.
Pardes Humanitarian Prize in Mental Health

1480. Can you name the politician who received the «Ernst Reuter Medal» in the year 1954?
James Bryant Conant

1481. Can you name the politician who received the «Manfred Wörner Medal» in the year 1996?
Richard Holbrooke

1482. Sheldon Whitehouse became a US senator from Rhode Island in the year 2017. Where was he born?
Manhattan

1483. Who replaced Joe Biden as the senator from Delaware in the year 1973?
Ted Kaufman

1484. Name any one award John Kenneth Galbraith received in the year 1994.
Lysenko Prize

1485. In which year did Charles Wesley Turnbull become the Governor of the United States Virgin Islands?
1999

1486. In the year 1987, whom did Tommy Thompson succeed as the Governor of Wisconsin?
Tony Earl

1487. In which year did Felix Perez Camacho become the Governor of Guam?
2003

1488. In which year did Ted Kennedy marry Joan Bennett Kennedy?
1958

1489. Where did Brian A. Smith get his bachelor's degree in agribusiness from?
Florida A&M University

1490. In which year did Hillary Clinton marry Bill Clinton?
1975

1491. Name any one award Louis Stokes received in the year 1999.
James Madison Award

1492. Joe Donnelly became a senator in the year 2015. Which state did he represent?
Indiana

1493. What medal did Barbara Jordan receive in the year 1992?
Spingarn Medal

1494. Whom did Albert II marry in the year 2011?
Charlene, Princess of Monaco

1495. In which year did Mark Dayton marry Alida Rockefeller Messinger?
1978

1496. Carl Levin became a US senator from Michigan in the year 1997. Where was he born?
Detroit

1497. Where was Jeff Sessions, a Republican senator from Alabama, born?
Selma

1498. Who replaced John Ensign as the senator from Nevada in the year 2001?
Dean Heller

1499. In the year 1983, whom did Richard Bryan succeed as the Governor of Nevada?
Robert List

1500. In which year did Bob Martinez become the Governor of Florida?
1987

1501. Can you name the politician who received the «Nobel Peace Prize» in the year 2002?
Jimmy Carter

1502. Name any one award Vannevar Bush received in the year 1953.
John J. Carty Award for the Advancement of Science

1503. Can you name the politician who received the «Peace Prize of Hesse» in the year 2008?
Sam Nunn

1504. Larry Craig became a US senator from Idaho in the year 1991. Where was he born?
Council

1505. What medal did David M. Kennedy receive in the year 2008?
Wilbur Cross Medal

1506. What is the name of Skip Humphrey's father?
Hubert Humphrey

1507. Can you name the politician who received the «Maxwell Finland Award» in the year 1996?
Paul Rogers

1508. In which year did Arnold Schwarzenegger marry Maria Shriver?
1986

1509. Can you name the politician who received the «University of Minnesota Distinguished McKnight University Professor» award in the year 2017?
Loren Terveen

1510. Where was Jean Carnahan, a senator from Missouri, born?
Washington, D.C.

1511. Who had hired Christopher Cox as an advisor in the year 1986?
Ronald Reagan

1512. Can you name the politician who received the «Giuseppe Motta Medal» in the year 2009?
Al Gore

1513. Can you name the politician who received the «Order of Aeronautical Merit» award in the year 1946?
Dwight D. Eisenhower

1514. Name any one award Louis Wade Sullivan received

in the year 1990.
Humanitarian of the Year

1515. In which year did Pat Quinn become the Governor of Illinois?
2009

1516. Jay Rockefeller became a US senator from West Virginia in the year 1995. Where was he born?
New York City

1517. Joe Lieberman became a US senator from Connecticut in the year 1993. Where was he born?
Stamford

1518. Where was Dick Durbin, a Democratic senator from Illinois, born?
East St. Louis

1519. Name any one award Steven Chu received in the year 1987.
Herbert P. Broida Award

1520. Name any one award Mary Mullarkey received in the year 2012.
Colorado Women's Hall of Fame

1521. In the year 1992, whom did Ed Schafer succeed as the Governor of North Dakota?
George Sinner

1522. Can you name the politician who received the «Sierra Club John Muir Award» in the year 1988?
John F. Seiberling

1523. Whom did Kent Conrad replace as the senator from North Dakota in the year 1987?

1524. Who replaced Jay Rockefeller as the senator from West Virginia in the year 1985?
Shelley Moore Capito

1525. Lisa Murkowski became a US senator from Alaska in the year 2013. Where was she born?
Ketchikan

1526. Name any one award Richard Nixon received in the year 1971.
Time Person of the Year

1527. Name any one award Arnold Schwarzenegger received in the year 2015.
WWE Hall of Fame

1528. Barbara Boxer became a US senator from California in the year 2015. Where was she born?
Brooklyn

1529. In the year 1973, whom did Philip W. Noel succeed as the Governor of Rhode Island?
Frank Licht

1530. Can you name the politician who received the «Golden Raspberry Award for Worst Screen Couple/Ensemble» in the year 2004?
George W. Bush

1531. Who replaced J. Bennett Johnston, Jr. as the senator from Louisiana in the year 1972?
Mary Landrieu

1532. In the year 1983, whom did Michael Dukakis succeed as the Governor of Massachusetts?

1533. David Karnes became a senator in the year 1987. Which state did he represent?
Nebraska

1534. What is the name of John Kasich's father?
John Kasich

1535. Where did Lawrence Summers get his doctorate degree in economics from?
Harvard University

1536. In which year did John G. Rowland become the Governor of Connecticut?
1995

1537. Where was Richard Blumenthal, a Democratic senator from Connecticut, born?
Brooklyn

1538. Name any one award George H. W. Bush received in the year 1990.
Doublespeak Award

1539. Where was Bill Nelson, a Democratic senator from Florida, born?
Miami

1540. In which year did Charlie Crist become the Governor of Florida?
2007

1541. In which year did Martin J. Schreiber become the Governor of Wisconsin?
1977

1542. What is the name of John McCain's father?
John S. McCain, Jr.

1543. In the year 2001, whom did Donald DiFrancesco succeed as the Governor of New Jersey?
Christine Todd Whitman

1544. What is the name of Jackie Chan's father?
Charles Chan

1545. From which university did John Thune get his Bachelor of Science degree in business?
Biola University

1546. Name any one award Barack Obama received in the year 2005.
Grammy Award for Best Spoken Word Album

1547. Who had hired Jaime Herrera Beutler as a member of congressional staff in the year 2005?
Cathy McMorris Rodgers

1548. Can you name the politician who received the «Congressional Activism Award» in the year 2015?
Bernie Sanders

1549. What medal did Rosalynn Carter get in the year 1999?
Presidential Medal of Freedom

1550. In which year did Paul E. Patton become the Governor of Kentucky?
1995

1551. Who replaced Mack Mattingly as the senator from Georgia in the year 1981?
Wyche Fowler

1552. Name any one award Tom Schieffer received in the year 2008.
Person of the Year, American Chamber of Commerce in Japan

1553. John Cornyn became a senator in the year 2003. Which state did he represent?
Texas

1554. In the year 2011, whom did Susana Martinez succeed as the Governor of New Mexico?
Bill Richardson

1555. Where did Janet Yellen get her Doctor of Philosophy degree in economics from?
Yale University

1556. What is the name of Sarah Sanders's mother?
Janet Huckabee

1557. Can you name the politician who received the «Computer Pioneer Award» in the year 1984?
Nathaniel Rochester

1558. In which year did Bill Graves become the Governor of Kansas?
1995

1559. Patrick Leahy became a US senator from Vermont in the year 2001. Where was he born?
Montpelier

1560. Can you name the politician who received the «Gallup's most admired man and woman poll» award in the year 1999?
Hillary Clinton

1561. In the year 1978, whom did John N. Dalton succeed as the Governor of Virginia?
Mills E. Godwin

1562. In the year 1987, whom did Joseph Franklin Ada succeed as the Governor of Guam?
Ricardo Bordallo

1563. Whom did Dee Dee Myers marry in the year 1997?
Todd Purdum

1564. Orrin Hatch, who belonged to the Republican Party, became a senator in the year 2015. Which state did he represent?
Utah

1565. Name any one award Hillary Clinton received in the year 2015.
Arkansas Women's Hall of Fame

1566. In the year 2003, whom did Sonny Perdue succeed as the Governor of Georgia?
Roy Barnes

1567. Whom did John Bailey marry in the year 1972?
Carol Littleton

1568. What medal did Robert Moses get in the year 1936?
Pugsley Medal

1569. Mary Landrieu became a US senator from Louisiana in the year 2001. Where was she born?
Arlington County

1570. In the year 2007, whom did Steve Beshear succeed as the Governor of Kentucky?

Ernie Fletcher

1571. Trent Lott, who belonged to the Republican Party, became a senator in the year 1997. Which state did he represent?
Mississippi

1572. Who had hired Daniel Lipinski as a member of congressional staff in the year 1999?
Rod Blagojevich

1573. Tim Johnson, who belonged to the Democratic Party, became a senator in the year 1999. Which state did he represent?
South Dakota

1574. What is the name of Patrick J. Kennedy's father?
Ted Kennedy

1575. Who replaced Jeffrey Chiesa as the senator from New Jersey in the year 2013?
Cory Booker

1576. Can you name the politician who received the «Alan T. Waterman Award» in the year 1987?
Lawrence Summers

1577. Can you name the politician who received the «Chicago Gay and Lesbian Hall of Fame» award in the year 2006?
Richard M. Daley

1578. Whom did Vincent Hughes marry in the year 2005?
Sheryl Lee Ralph

1579. In which year did Michael Bloomberg marry Susan Brown?

1580. What is the name of David Miliband's father?
Ralph Miliband

1581. Name any one award Ronald Reagan received in the year 1969.
Horatio Alger Award

1582. In the year 2005, whom did Jon Huntsman, Jr. succeed as the Governor of Utah?
Olene S. Walker

1583. Sheldon Whitehouse became a senator in the year 2013. Which state did he represent?
Rhode Island

1584. What is the name of Nancy Vaughan's father?
Fred Barakat

1585. Who had hired Gerry Studds as an employee in the year 1962?
John F. Kennedy

1586. Can you name the politician who received the «Grand Cross of Order of Manuel Amador Guerrero» award in the year 2001?
Howard Baker

1587. Russ Feingold, who belonged to the Democratic Party, became a senator in the year 2007. Which state did he represent?
Wisconsin

1588. Tim Johnson, who belonged to the Democratic Party, became a senator in the year 2005. Which state did he represent?

South Dakota

1589. What is the name of Albert II's father?
Rainier III

1590. Name any one award Ayaan Hirsi Ali received in the year 2008.
Anisfield-Wolf Book Awards

1591. From which university did Sammuel Sanes get his Bachelor of Arts degree in public administration?
Florida Memorial University

1592. Where did Conor Lamb get his Bachelor of Arts degree in political science from?
University of Pennsylvania

1593. Name any one award Lynn Swann received in the year 1981.
Walter Payton Man of the Year Award

1594. In which year did Linda Lingle become the Governor of Hawaii?
2002

1595. In the year 1994, whom did Tony Knowles succeed as the Governor of Alaska?
Wally Hickel

1596. Can you name the politician who received the «Maine Women's Hall of Fame» award in the year 2008?
Karen Heck

1597. What medal did Barbara Jordan get in the year 1994?
Presidential Medal of Freedom

1598. In the year 1972, whom did Jere Beasley succeed as the Governor of Alabama?
George Wallace

1599. Whom did Caroline Kennedy marry in the year 1986?
Edwin Schlossberg

1600. Name any one award Daniel Kemmis received in the year 1996.
Charles Frankel Prize

1601. Carol Moseley Braun became a US senator from Illinois in the year 1995. Where was she born?
Chicago

1602. What medal did James R. Thompson receive in the year 1991?
Holley Medal

1603. Who had hired Randy Hultgren as a member of congressional staff in the year 1988?
Dennis Hastert

1604. In which year did William Weld become the Governor of Massachusetts?
1991

1605. Where was Lisa Murkowski, a Republican senator from Alaska, born?
Ketchikan

1606. What medal did Madeleine Albright get in the year 2012?
Presidential Medal of Freedom

1607. In which year did Pat McCrory become the Governor

of North Carolina?
2013

1608. Name any one award Kevin Johnson received in the year 1989.
NBA Most Improved Player Award

1609. Who had hired Paul Ryan as a member of congressional staff in the year 1995?
Sam Brownback

1610. Whom did George Voinovich replace as the senator from Ohio in the year 1999?
John Glenn

1611. In which year did Lawrence Lau marry Ayesha Macpherson?
2010

1612. In which year did Bill Haslam become the Governor of Tennessee?
2011

1613. In which year did Joe Scarborough marry Mika Brzezinski?
2018

1614. In the year 2005, whom did Mitch Daniels succeed as the Governor of Indiana?
Joe E. Kernan

1615. In the year 1979, Bart Gordon worked as a director in which political party?
Tennessee Democratic Party

1616. Can you name the politician who received the «Knight Grand Cross with Collar of the Order of Merit of

the Italian Republic» award in the year 2005?
Albert II

1617. Name any one award Jan Schakowsky received in the year 2015.
Chicago Gay and Lesbian Hall of Fame

1618. Whom did Bill Clinton marry in the year 1975?
Hillary Clinton

1619. What is the name of Ivanka Trump's mother?
Ivana Trump

1620. What medal did Yehudi Menuhin get in the year 1981?
Albert Medal

1621. Where was Tom Harkin, a Democratic senator from Iowa, born?
Warren County

1622. Who had hired Ruben Kihuen as a member of congressional staff in the year 2004?
Harry Reid

1623. What medal did Herbert A. Simon receive in the year 1986?
National Medal of Science

1624. Can you name the politician who received the «Charlemagne Prize» in the year 1987?
Henry Kissinger

1625. In which year did Chris Christie become the Governor of New Jersey?
2010

1626. What is the name of Marco Rubio's father?
Mario Rubio

1627. Name any one award Bill Clinton received in the year 2011.
Grand Cross of the National Order of Honor and Merit

1628. Who had hired Carte Goodwin as a general counsel in the year 2005?
Joe Manchin

1629. Can you name the politician who received the «Francis Boyer Award» in the year 1985?
Jeane Kirkpatrick

1630. In the year 1973, whom did Thomas Lee Judge succeed as the Governor of Montana?
Forrest H. Anderson

1631. Tom Coburn became a US senator from Oklahoma in the year 2007. Where was he born?
Casper

1632. Where was Chris Dodd, a Democratic senator from Connecticut, born?
Willimantic

1633. Can you name the politician who received the «American Defense Service Medal» in the year 1945?
John F. Kennedy

1634. Can you name the politician who received the «Lucy Award» in the year 1997?
Roseanne Barr

1635. Name any one award Joe Biden received in the year 2008.

1636. Herb Kohl, who belonged to the Democratic Party, became a senator in the year 1999. Which state did he represent?
Wisconsin

1637. Where was Roger Wicker, a Republican senator from Mississippi, born?
Pontotoc

1638. Where was Chris Coons, a Democratic senator from Delaware, born?
Greenwich

1639. Can you name the politician who received the «Theodore Roosevelt Award» in the year 1999?
Bill Richardson

1640. Who replaced Dan Coats as the senator from Indiana in the year 1989?
Evan Bayh

1641. What is the name of Ben Quayle's father?
Dan Quayle

1642. Where did Laurie Halverson get her Bachelor of Science degree in political science from?
St. Catherine University

1643. Who replaced William Cohen as the senator from Maine in the year 1979?
Susan Collins

1644. Whom did Norm Coleman replace as the senator from Minnesota in the year 2003?
Dean Barkley

1645. Name any one award Margaret Chase Smith received in the year 2007.
Distinguished Americans series

1646. Whom did Dennis Kucinich marry in the year 2005?
Elizabeth Kucinich

1647. Can you name the politician who received the «Hoover Medal» in the year 1970?
J. Erik Jonsson

1648. Where was Jim Risch, a Republican senator from Idaho, born?
Milwaukee

1649. In the year 2012, Ro Khanna was a member of which government agency?
California Labor and Workforce Development Agency

1650. Name any one award Ted Kennedy received in the year 2008.
Order of the Aztec Eagle

1651. What medal did George F. Kennan get in the year 1989?
Presidential Medal of Freedom

1652. Can you name the politician who received the «Michigan Women's Hall of Fame» award in the year 1988?
Agnes Mary Mansour

1653. Whom did Jared Kushner marry in the year 2009?
Ivanka Trump

1654. Elizabeth Dole became a US senator from North

Carolina in the year 2003. Where was she born?
Salisbury

1655. Whom did Dirk Kempthorne replace as the senator from Idaho in the year 1993?
Steve Symms

1656. Whom did Karin Housley marry in the year 1985?
Phil Housley

1657. Can you name the politician who received the «Officer of the Order of Canada» award in the year 1984?
Stanley Knowles

1658. In which year did Donald Trump marry Marla Maples?
1993

1659. In the year 1990, whom did James Florio succeed as the Governor of New Jersey?
Thomas Kean

1660. From which university did Karen Pence get her Master of Science degree in primary education?
Butler University

1661. In which year did Jerry Weller marry Zury Ríos?
2004

1662. Name any one award Hubert Humphrey received in the year 1977.
Freedom Award

1663. Susan Collins became a US senator from Maine in the year 2003. Where was she born?
Caribou

1664. Where was Bernie Sanders, a senator from Vermont, born?
Brooklyn

1665. In which year did Robert P. Casey become the Governor of Pennsylvania?
1987

1666. In which year did Brad Henry become the Governor of Oklahoma?
2003

1667. In which year did Christopher Guest marry Jamie Lee Curtis?
1984

1668. Where did Joe Biden get his Bachelor of Science degree in study of history from?
University of Delaware

1669. In which year did Kenneth Mapp become the Governor of the United States Virgin Islands?
2015

1670. Jim Mountain Inhofe became a US senator from Oklahoma in the year 1997. Where was he born?
Des Moines

1671. Can you name the politician who received the «honorary doctor of the Hebrew University of Jerusalem» award in the year 1989?
Daniel Inouye

1672. In the year 1981, Tom Campbell worked as a director in which government agency?
Federal Trade Commission

1673. Name any one award Eleanor Roosevelt received in the year 1973.
National Women's Hall of Fame

1674. Whom did Zell Miller replace as the senator from Georgia in the year 2000?
Paul Coverdell

1675. Can you name the politician who received the «American Peace Award» in the year 2009?
Jimmy Carter

1676. Jay Rockefeller became a senator in the year 2005. Which state did he represent?
West Virginia

1677. From which university did Angela Angel get her Bachelor of Arts degree in political science?
Hampton University

1678. Name any one award William Cohen received in the year 2001.
Theodore Roosevelt Award

1679. Where was Sam Brownback, a Republican senator from Kansas, born?
Garnett

1680. Paul Tsongas became a US senator from Massachusetts in the year 1979. Where was he born?
Lowell

1681. Where was Kent Conrad, a Democratic senator from North Dakota, born?
Bismarck

1682. Where was Kaneaster Hodges, a senator from

Arkansas, born?
Newport

1683. Can you name the politician who received the «Francis Boyer Award» in the year 2001?
Clarence Thomas

1684. Name any one award Hillary Clinton received in the year 2014.
William O. Douglas Award

1685. Whom did John Kerry marry in the year 1995?
Teresa Heinz Kerry

1686. Can you name the politician who received the «Order of the Royal House of Chakri» award in the year 1960?
Dwight D. Eisenhower

1687. Name any one award Nancy Pelosi received in the year 2019.
Profile in Courage Award

1688. What medal did Jesse Helms get in the year 2001?
Truman-Reagan Medal of Freedom

1689. What is the name of Clay Aiken's father?
Vernon Grissom

1690. Jon Tester became a senator in the year 2017. Which state did he represent?
Montana

1691. Jeff Sessions, who belonged to the Republican Party, became a senator in the year 2015. Which state did he represent?
Alabama

1692. Whom did James Brady marry in the year 1973?
Sarah Brady

1693. Can you name the politician who received the «Ig Nobel Prize» in the year 2011?
Pat Robertson

1694. Name any one award Dave Bing received in the year 1971.
All-NBA Team

1695. Name any one award Patsy Mink received in the year 2003.
National Women's Hall of Fame

1696. What is the name of Bill Clinton's mother?
Virginia Clinton Kelley

1697. Chris Dodd became a senator in the year 2009. Which state did he represent?
Connecticut

1698. Name any one award Gerald Ford received in the year 1977.
Francis Boyer Award

1699. Can you name the politician who received the «NAACP Image Award – Chairman's Award» in the year 2005?
Barack Obama

1700. Who became the mayor of Nashville in the year 2015?
Megan Barry

1701. Can you name the politician who received the

«Colorado Women's Hall of Fame» award in the year 2000?
Polly Baca

1702. Mazie Hirono became a senator in the year 2013. Which state did she represent?
Hawaii

1703. Where was Jake Garn, a Republican senator from Utah, born?
Richfield

1704. Name any one award Betty Ford received in the year 2013.
National Women's Hall of Fame

1705. Who had hired Daniel Lipinski as a member of congressional staff in the year 1993?
George E. Sangmeister

1706. Where did Donald Trump get his Bachelor of Science degree in economics from?
The Wharton School

1707. Tom Coburn became a senator in the year 2005. Which state did he represent?
Oklahoma

1708. Can you name the politician who received the «Chicago Gay and Lesbian Hall of Fame» award in the year 2014?
Kelly Cassidy

1709. Whom did Dennis Kucinich marry in the year 1977?
Sandra Lee McCarthy

1710. Frank Murkowski became a US senator from Alaska

in the year 1995. Where was he born?
Seattle

1711. Richard Blumenthal became a US senator from Connecticut in the year 2017. Where was he born?
Brooklyn

1712. Maria Cantwell became a US senator from Washington in the year 2005. Where was she born?
Indianapolis

1713. In the year 2001, whom did Judy Martz succeed as the Governor of Montana?
Marc Racicot

1714. Can you name the politician who received the «American Book Awards» in the year 1998?
Angela Davis

1715. In the year 1994, whom did Christine Todd Whitman succeed as the Governor of New Jersey?
James Florio

1716. Who had hired Zoe Lofgren as a member of congressional staff in the year 1970?
Don Edwards

1717. Kay Hagan became a US senator from North Carolina in the year 2011. Where was she born?
Shelby

1718. Can you name the politician who received the «Benjamin Franklin Medal» in the year 1999?
George John Mitchell Jr.

1719. Harry Reid became a US senator from Nevada in the year 1999. Where was he born?

Searchlight

1720. What medal did Seth Moulton receive in the year 2003?
Commendation Medal

1721. Whom did David Petraeus marry in the year 1974?
Holly Knowlton

1722. What is the name of Jim Doyle's father?
James Edward Doyle

1723. Whom did Paul G. Kirk replace as the senator from Massachusetts in the year 2009?
Ted Kennedy

1724. In which year did Jay Nixon become the Governor of Missouri?
2009

1725. Whom did Maxine Waters marry in the year 1977?
Sid Williams

1726. Name any one award Oveta Culp Hobby received in the year 1996.
National Women's Hall of Fame

1727. In the year 1997, George Voinovich worked as a chairperson in which organization?
National Governors Association

1728. In the year 1998, Tom Carper worked as a chairperson in which organization?
National Governors Association

1729. Name any one award Norman Thomas received in the year 1967.

1730. Can you name the politician who received the «Presidential Medal of Freedom» in the year 2008?
Ben Carson

1731. John McCain, who belonged to the Republican Party, became a senator in the year 2005. Which state did he represent?
Arizona

1732. Where was Lincoln Chafee, a Republican senator from Rhode Island, born?
Warwick

1733. Where was Mel Martinez, a Republican senator from Florida, born?
Sagua La Grande

1734. Can you name the politician who received the «IJCAI Award for Research Excellence» in the year 1995?
Herbert A. Simon

1735. In which year did Bill de Blasio marry Chirlane McCray?
1994

1736. Tim Scott became a senator in the year 2017. Which state did he represent?
South Carolina

1737. Mark Warner became a senator in the year 2011. Which state did he represent?
Virginia

1738. In which year did Madeleine M. Kunin become the Governor of Vermont?

1985

1739. In which year did Mike Hayden become the Governor of Kansas?
1987

1740. Name any one award Franklin Delano Roosevelt received in the year 1941.
Time Person of the Year

1741. Whom did Tim Johnson replace as the senator from South Dakota in the year 1997?
Larry Pressler

1742. What medal did Herbert Hoover get in the year 1920?
Public Welfare Medal

1743. Can you name the politician who received the «Medal of Honor» in the year 2001?
Theodore Roosevelt

1744. Name any one award Helen Delich Bentley received in the year 2006.
International Maritime Hall of Fame

1745. In which year did Mel Carnahan become the Governor of Missouri?
1993

1746. Whom did Fred Thompson replace as the senator from Tennessee in the year 1994?
Harlan Mathews

1747. Whom did Mitch McConnell marry in the year 1993?
Elaine Chao

1748. Mark Pryor became a senator in the year 2005. Which state did he represent?
Arkansas

1749. Who had hired Ann McLane Kuster as a member of congressional staff in the year 1978?
Pete McCloskey

1750. Who replaced Larry Pressler as the senator from South Dakota in the year 1979?
Tim Johnson

1751. Jim Talent became a senator in the year 2005. Which state did he represent?
Missouri

1752. Where was Daniel S. Sullivan, a Republican senator from Alaska, born?
Fairview Park

1753. Can you name the politician who received the «Candace Award» in the year 1989?
Condoleezza Rice

1754. In which year did Thomas Kean become the Governor of New Jersey?
1982

1755. Barbara Mikulski became a senator in the year 1993. Which state did she represent?
Maryland

1756. Roger Wicker became a senator in the year 2009. Which state did he represent?
Mississippi

1757. In which year did Dan Quayle marry Marilyn

Quayle?
1972

1758. David Pryor became a US senator from Arkansas in the year 1979. Where was he born?
Camden

1759. In which year did John de Jongh become the Governor of the United States Virgin Islands?
2007

1760. Name any one award Edward M. Kennedy, Jr. received in the year 2008.
honorary doctor of Harvard University

1761. Paul Sarbanes became a senator in the year 1999. Which state did he represent?
Maryland

1762. Can you name the politician who received the «Elizabeth Blackwell Award» in the year 2015?
Janet Yellen

1763. What is the name of Susan Collins's father?
Donald Collins

1764. Can you name the politician who received the «Rhodes Scholarship» award in the year 1950?
Richard Lugar

1765. Can you name the politician who received the «Harold W. McGraw Prize in Education» in the year 1999?
Jim Hunt

1766. Can you name the politician who received the «Langley Gold Medal» in the year 1976?
James E. Webb

1767. In which year did Joe Lieberman marry Hadassah Lieberman?
1982

1768. Can you name the politician who received the «NBA Rookie of the Year Award» in the year 1967?
Dave Bing

1769. In the year 1981, Bart Gordon worked as a chairperson in which political party?
Tennessee Democratic Party

1770. What is the name of Jiří Dienstbier Jr.'s mother?
Zuzana Dienstbierová

1771. Paul Coverdell became a senator in the year 1995. Which state did he represent?
Georgia

1772. What is the name of Kathleen Kennedy Townsend's mother?
Ethel Skakel Kennedy

1773. Can you name the politician who received the «Golden Raspberry Award for Worst Actor» in the year 2004?
George W. Bush

1774. Name any one award John Glenn received in the year 1999.
Princess of Asturias Award for International Cooperation

1775. Who replaced Jon Corzine as the senator from New Jersey in the year 2001?
Robert Menendez

1776. What is the name of Beau Biden's father?
Joe Biden

1777. In which year did Mark White become the Governor of Texas?
1983

1778. Max Baucus became a senator in the year 1995. Which state did he represent?
Montana

1779. Can you name the politician who received the «Grand Cross special issue of the Order of Merit of the Federal Republic of Germany, special issue» award in the year 1993?
George H. W. Bush

1780. Maria Cantwell, who belonged to the Democratic Party, became a senator in the year 2017. Which state did she represent?
Washington

1781. Lamar Alexander became a US senator from Tennessee in the year 2005. Where was he born?
Maryville

1782. Can you name the politician who received the «Chatham House Prize» in the year 2013?
Hillary Clinton

1783. Can you name the politician who received the «ASCB Public Service Award» in the year 2014?
Rush D. Holt, Jr.

1784. Can you name the politician who received the «Freedom Award» in the year 1969?
Lucius D. Clay

1785. Where was Frank Murkowski, a Republican senator from Alaska, born?
Seattle

1786. Name any one award Henry Kissinger received in the year 2005.
honorary doctor of the Peking University

1787. Who had hired Bob Goodlatte as a member of congressional staff in the year 1977?
M. Caldwell Butler

1788. What is the name of Shelley Moore Capito's father?
Arch A. Moore

1789. Can you name the politician who received the «National Academy of Engineering Founders Award» in the year 1966?
Vannevar Bush

1790. Where did Aftab Pureval work as a student government president in the year 2004?
Ohio State University

1791. Who replaced John Walsh as the senator from Montana in the year 2014?
Steve Daines

1792. Can you name the politician who received the «Master of Sport of the USSR» award in the year 1987?
Anatoly Kashpirovsky

1793. Name any one award Alan Page received in the year 1971.
National Football League Most Valuable Player Award

1794. Whom did Butch Otter marry in the year 2006?
Lori Easley

1795. In which year did Barbara Roberts become the Governor of Oregon?
1991

1796. In the year 1979, Steven Schiff worked as City attorney in which law enforcement agency?
Albuquerque Police Department

1797. Name any one award Frank Lautenberg received in the year 1990.
James Madison Award

1798. John F. Reed became a US senator from Rhode Island in the year 2007. Where was he born?
Providence

1799. John Breaux became a senator in the year 1993. Which state did he represent?
Louisiana

1800. Name any one award Charlotta Bass received in the year 2014.
California Hall of Fame

1801. In which year did Sam Brownback become the Governor of Kansas?
2011

1802. Can you name the politician who received the «Josiah Willard Gibbs Lectureship» award in the year 1935?
Vannevar Bush

1803. Jon Kyl became a US senator from Arizona in the

year 1999. Where was he born?
Oakland

1804. In the year 1969, Richard Blumenthal worked as a helper in which organization?
White House Office

1805. Bill Bradley, who belonged to the Democratic Party, became a senator in the year 1993. Which state did he represent?
New Jersey

1806. Steve Symms became a US senator from Idaho in the year 1991. Where was he born?
Nampa

1807. In the year 1991, whom did Zell Miller succeed as the Governor of Georgia?
Joe Frank Harris

1808. Can you name the politician who received the «National Women's Hall of Fame» award in the year 2005?
Patricia Locke

1809. Name any one award Harold Jefferson Coolidge, Jr. received in the year 1980.
J. Paul Getty Award for Conservation Leadership

1810. Where was Barbara Mikulski, a Democratic senator from Maryland, born?
Baltimore

1811. Where was Ed Markey, a Democratic senator from Massachusetts, born?
Malden

1812. Can you name the politician who received the

«Order of Liberty» award in the year 2016?
Richard Lugar

1813. Can you name the politician who received the «Gallup's most admired man and woman poll» award in the year 1993?
Hillary Clinton

1814. Harry Reid became a US senator from Nevada in the year 1991. Where was he born?
Searchlight

1815. Judd Gregg became a US senator from New Hampshire in the year 2005. Where was he born?
Nashua

1816. Can you name the politician who received the «National Medal of Science» in the year 1973?
John Tukey

1817. Can you name the politician who received the «Heinz Award» in the year 1999?
Daniel Patrick Moynihan

1818. Olympia Snowe became a US senator from Maine in the year 2003. Where was she born?
Augusta

1819. Name any one award George P. Shultz received in the year 2007.
honorary doctor of the Peking University

1820. James Abourezk became a senator in the year 1973. Which state did he represent?
South Dakota

1821. In which year did Frank Murkowski become the

Governor of Alaska?
2002

1822. Can you name the politician who received the «John Simon Guggenheim Memorial Foundation Fellowship» award in the year 1986?
Janet Yellen

1823. In the year 1982, Hillary Clinton worked as a board member in which nonprofit organization?
New World Foundation

1824. Can you name the politician who received the «Great Cross with Star and Sash of the Order of Merit of the Federal Republic of Germany» award in the year 2013?
Richard Lugar

1825. Can you name the politician who received the «Ernst von Siemens Music Prize» in the year 1984?
Yehudi Menuhin

1826. Can you name the politician who received the «ASCB Public Service Award» in the year 2000?
Donna Shalala

1827. Who became the mayor of Oakland in the year 1991?
Elihu Harris

1828. Can you name the politician who received the «Nobel Peace Prize» in the year 2009?
Barack Obama

1829. Can you name the politician who received the «Deshikottam» award in the year 1952?
Eleanor Roosevelt

1830. Can you name the politician who received the «Person of the Year, American Chamber of Commerce in Japan» award in the year 2004?
Howard Baker

1831. In the year 2003, whom did Mike Rounds succeed as the Governor of South Dakota?
Bill Janklow

1832. Mike DeWine became a US senator from Ohio in the year 1999. Where was he born?
Springfield

1833. What is the name of Jiří Dienstbier Jr.'s father?
Jiří Dienstbier

1834. Richard Shelby became a senator in the year 2007. Which state did he represent?
Alabama

1835. Name any one award Rita Levi-Montalcini received in the year 1983.
Louisa Gross Horwitz Prize

1836. In which year did Wendell Anderson become the Governor of Minnesota?
1971

1837. Todd Young became a US senator from Indiana in the year 2017. Where was he born?
Lancaster

1838. Where did Jack Collins get his Bachelor of Arts degree in natural sciences from?
Rowan University

1839. Can you name the politician who received the «Order of Playa Girón» award in the year 1972?
Angela Davis

1840. What medal did Tom McCall receive in the year 1974?
Audubon Medal

1841. In the year 2001, Jared Huffman worked as a lawyer in which environmental organization?
Natural Resources Defense Council

1842. From which college did John Roberts get his Bachelor of Arts degree in study of history?
Harvard College

1843. In the year 1981, whom did Kit Bond succeed as the Governor of Missouri?
Joseph P. Teasdale

1844. Can you name the politician who received the «Horatio Alger Award» in the year 1992?
Clarence Thomas

1845. Whom did Kevin Johnson marry in the year 2011?
Michelle Rhee

1846. Where was Lamar Alexander, a Republican senator from Tennessee, born?
Maryville

1847. In the year 2000, Will Hurd worked as a chief operating officer in which intelligence agency?
Central Intelligence Agency

1848. In the year 1971, Jim Leach worked as a delegate in which intergovernmental organization?

United Nations

1849. Sam Brownback became a senator in the year 2003. Which state did he represent?
Kansas

1850. What medal did Jimmy Carter receive in the year 1979?
International Mediation medal

1851. In which year did William Weld marry Susan Roosevelt Weld?
1975

1852. Where did John Marty get his Bachelor of Arts degree in ethics from?
St. Olaf College

1853. What is the name of Beau Biden's mother?
Neilia Hunter

1854. Joe Manchin became a senator in the year 2015. Which state did he represent?
West Virginia

1855. Can you name the politician who received the «Charles Frankel Prize» in the year 1991?
Winton M. Blount

1856. In the year 2010, whom did Neil Abercrombie succeed as the Governor of Hawaii?
Linda Lingle

1857. In which year did Chuck Morse become the Governor of New Hampshire?
2017

1858. Mark Pryor became a senator in the year 2011. Which state did he represent?
Arkansas

1859. From which college did Edwin Erickson get his Doctor of Philosophy degree in biochemistry?
Bryn Mawr College

1860. In which year did Frank Keating become the Governor of Oklahoma?
1995

1861. Name any one award Ayaan Hirsi Ali received in the year 2006.
The glass of reason

1862. Name any one award John Martinis received in the year 2014.
Fritz London Memorial Prizes

1863. In which year did Tulsi Gabbard marry Abraham Williams?
2015

1864. In the year 1987, whom did Cecil D. Andrus succeed as the Governor of Idaho?
John V. Evans

1865. Whom did Jay Rockefeller marry in the year 1967?
Sharon Percy Rockefeller

1866. Whom did Kay Bailey Hutchison replace as the senator from Texas in the year 1993?
Bob Krueger

1867. Whom did Frank G. Wisner marry in the year 1976?
Christine de Ganay

1868. Where did Boyd K. Rutherford get his master's degree in communication studies from?
USC Annenberg School for Communication and Journalism

1869. Richard Lugar became a senator in the year 2003. Which state did he represent?
Indiana

1870. Can you name the politician who received the «Labor Hall of Honor» award in the year 2015?
Ted Kennedy

1871. Barbara Mikulski became a senator in the year 1991. Which state did she represent?
Maryland

1872. Where was Debbie Stabenow, a Democratic senator from Michigan, born?
Gladwin

1873. In the year 1989, whom did Gaston Caperton succeed as the Governor of West Virginia?
Arch A. Moore

1874. What is the name of Alison Lundergan Grimes's father?
Jerry Lundergan

1875. From which university did Melvin Carter III get his bachelor's degree in business administration?
Florida A&M University

1876. What is the name of Madeleine Albright's mother?
Anna Spiegelova

1877. Richard Shelby, who belonged to the Republican

Party, became a senator in the year 1995. Which state did he represent?
Alabama

1878. Chuck Robb, who belonged to the Democratic Party, became a senator in the year 1995. Which state did he represent?
Virginia

1879. In the year 1983, whom did Mario Cuomo succeed as the Governor of New York?
Hugh Carey

1880. In which year did Jay Carney marry Claire Shipman?
2001

1881. In which year did David Pryor become the Governor of Arkansas?
1975

1882. In the year 1999, whom did Don Siegelman succeed as the Governor of Alabama?
Forrest Hood James, Jr.

1883. Who replaced Al D'Amato as the senator from New York in the year 1981?
Charles Ellis Schumer

1884. Name any one award Angela Davis received in the year 2011.
Blue Planet Award

1885. John Cornyn became a senator in the year 2007. Which state did he represent?
Texas

1886. In which year did Jeanne Shaheen become the Governor of New Hampshire?
1997

1887. Where did Hillary Clinton get her Bachelor of Arts degree in political science from?
Wellesley College

1888. Can you name the politician who received the «National Medal of Science» in the year 1963?
Vannevar Bush

1889. Bob Corker, who belonged to the Republican Party, became a senator in the year 2011. Which state did he represent?
Tennessee

1890. In which year did Dirk Kempthorne become the Governor of Idaho?
1999

1891. In the year 2006, whom did Jim Risch succeed as the Governor of Idaho?
Dirk Kempthorne

1892. In the year 1986, whom did John D. Waihee III succeed as the Governor of Hawaii?
George Ariyoshi

1893. Who replaced Nancy Landon Kassebaum as the senator from Kansas in the year 1978?
Pat Roberts

1894. Whom did Anthony Weiner marry in the year 2010?
Huma Abedin

1895. Name any one award Barack Obama received in the

year 2008.
Time Person of the Year

1896. Can you name the politician who received the «International Freedom Conductor Award» in the year 2013?
Fred Shuttlesworth

1897. Where was Carl Levin, a Democratic senator from Michigan, born?
Detroit

1898. From which university did Mikie Sherrill get her professional certification degree in Arabic?
The American University in Cairo

1899. Tom Daschle became a US senator from South Dakota in the year 1987. Where was he born?
Aberdeen

1900. Ron Lee Wyden became a senator in the year 2017. Which state did he represent?
Oregon

1901. What medal did Wilson Riles get in the year 1973?
Spingarn Medal

1902. Ron Lee Wyden, who belonged to the Democratic Party, became a senator in the year 2009. Which state did he represent?
Oregon

1903. What is the name of Kathleen Kennedy Townsend's father?
Robert F. Kennedy

1904. What is the name of Madeleine Albright's father?

Josef Korbel

1905. Whom did Wendell Anderson replace as the senator from Minnesota in the year 1976?
Walter Mondale

1906. In the year 1972, John Spratt worked as a delegate in which political party?
South Carolina Democratic Party

1907. Name any one award Elly M. Peterson received in the year 1984.
Michigan Women's Hall of Fame

1908. In the year 1991, Kevin Cramer worked as the party chair in which political party?
North Dakota Republican Party

1909. Name any one award Oren Harris received in the year 1963.
Lasker-Bloomberg Public Service Award

1910. Robert Menendez became a senator in the year 2007. Which state did he represent?
New Jersey

1911. Can you name the politician who received the «Heinz Award» in the year 2004?
Richard Lugar

1912. Name any one award James Wolfensohn received in the year 1995.
Knight Commander of the Order of the British Empire

1913. What medal did Alben W. Barkley receive in the year 1949?
Congressional Gold Medal

1914. Bill Bradley became a US senator from New Jersey in the year 1991. Where was he born?
Crystal City

1915. Name any one award Henry Kissinger received in the year 1975.
Wateler Peace Prize

1916. Name any one award Betty Ford received in the year 1987.
Michigan Women's Hall of Fame

1917. Where was John Breaux, a Democratic senator from Louisiana, born?
Crowley

1918. Barbara Boxer became a US senator from California in the year 1993. Where was she born?
Brooklyn

1919. Wyche Fowler became a US senator from Georgia in the year 1987. Where was he born?
Atlanta

1920. In the year 2009, whom did Jack Markell succeed as the Governor of Delaware?
Ruth Ann Minner

1921. Can you name the politician who received the «Langley Gold Medal» in the year 1987?
Barry Goldwater

1922. Whom did John Grisham marry in the year 1981?
Renee Grisham

1923. Name any one award Angela Davis received in the

year 2006.
Thomas Merton Award

1924. Thad Cochran, who belonged to the Republican Party, became a senator in the year 1999. Which state did he represent?
Mississippi

1925. In the year 1979, whom did Joseph E. Brennan succeed as the Governor of Maine?
James B. Longley

1926. Name any one award Mike Quigley received in the year 2009.
Chicago Gay and Lesbian Hall of Fame

1927. In the year 1978, Hillary Clinton worked as a chairperson in which nonprofit organization?
Legal Services Corporation

1928. In which year did Richard Codey become the Governor of New Jersey?
2004

1929. John F. Reed, who belonged to the Democratic Party, became a senator in the year 2005. Which state did he represent?
Rhode Island

1930. From which university did Bernie Sanders get his Bachelor of Arts degree in political science?
University of Chicago

1931. In which year did Beto O'Rourke marry Amy O'Rourke?
2005

1932. Orrin Hatch became a senator in the year 1999. Which state did he represent?
Utah

1933. Kay Bailey Hutchison, who belonged to the Republican Party, became a senator in the year 2003. Which state did she represent?
Texas

1934. Can you name the politician who received the «Jewish National Fund Tree of Life Award» in the year 1983?
Donald Trump

1935. Can you name the politician who received the «Warren Christopher Public Service Award» in the year 2013?
Hillary Clinton

1936. What is the name of Hillary Clinton's mother?
Dorothy Howell Rodham

1937. Can you name the politician who received the «honorary degree» award in the year 2014?
Albert II

1938. Ben Nelson became a US senator from Nebraska in the year 2001. Where was he born?
McCook

1939. Bill Frist became a US senator from Tennessee in the year 1999. Where was he born?
Nashville

1940. Name any one award Steven Chu received in the year 1993.
King Faisal International Prize in Science

1941. J. Bennett Johnston, Jr. became a senator in the year 1995. Which state did he represent?
Louisiana

1942. Can you name the politician who received the «Philadelphia Liberty Medal» in the year 2013?
Hillary Clinton

1943. Who became the mayor of Richmond in the year 2007?
Gayle McLaughlin

1944. John Cornyn, who belonged to the Republican Party, became a senator in the year 2011. Which state did he represent?
Texas

1945. Who had hired Jackie Speier as a member of congressional staff in the year 1973?
Leo Ryan

1946. Kay Bailey Hutchison became a US senator from Texas in the year 2011. Where was she born?
Galveston

1947. Where was Tammy Baldwin, a Democratic senator from Wisconsin, born?
Madison

1948. In which year did Richard Lamm become the Governor of Colorado?
1975

1949. Where was Ted Kennedy, a senator from Massachusetts, born?
Boston

1950. Name any one award Dave Bing received in the year 1976.
NBA All-Star Game Most Valuable Player Award

1951. Where did Paul G. Kirk work as a treasurer in the year 1983?
Democratic National Committee

1952. Patty Murray became a US senator from Washington in the year 2011. Where was she born?
Seattle

1953. Whom did Paul Sarbanes replace as the senator from Maryland in the year 1977?
John Glenn Beall Jr.

1954. What medal did Vannevar Bush receive in the year 1945?
Public Welfare Medal

1955. Whom did Clarence Thomas marry in the year 1971?
Kathy Ambush

1956. Can you name the politician who received the «Wallenberg Medal» in the year 1999?
John Lewis

1957. Can you name the politician who received the «Walter Payton Man of the Year Award» in the year 1988?
Steve Largent

1958. In the year 1991, whom did Fife Symington III succeed as the Governor of Arizona?
Rose Mofford

1959. Can you name the politician who received the

«Freedom Award» in the year 1995?
Richard Holbrooke

1960. What medal did James Bryant Conant receive in the year 1944?
Priestley Medal

1961. Who wrote the book «Night Comes to the Cumberlands»?
Harry M. Caudill

1962. In the year 1993, Paul Ryan worked as an employee in which organization?
FreedomWorks

1963. From which university did Andy Beshear get his bachelor's degree in political science?
Vanderbilt University

1964. Can you name the politician who received the «Doublespeak Award» in the year 1980?
Ronald Reagan

1965. Whom did Frank Hibbard replace as the mayor of Clearwater in the year 2005?
George Cretekos

1966. Dianne Feinstein, who belonged to the Democratic Party, became a senator in the year 1993. Which state did she represent?
California

1967. Can you name the politician who received the «Pugsley Medal» in the year 1948?
Percival Proctor Baxter

1968. Can you name the politician who received the «John

Scott Medal» in the year 1943?
Vannevar Bush

1969. Where did Tim Kaine work as a chairperson in the year 2009?
Democratic National Committee

1970. What is the name of Bill Clinton's father?
William Jefferson Blythe, Jr.

1971. In which year did Booth Gardner become the Governor of Washington?
1985

1972. Can you name the politician who received the «American Peace Award» in the year 2008?
Cindy Sheehan

1973. In which year did Martin O'Malley become the Governor of Maryland?
2007

1974. Can you name the politician who received the «Dana Award for Pioneering Achievement in Health and Education» in the year 1986?
Nancy Reagan

1975. In which year did Jim Hodges become the Governor of South Carolina?
1999

1976. Can you name the politician who received the «Horatio Alger Award» in the year 2011?
Michael Bloomberg

1977. Whom did Gabrielle Giffords marry in the year 2007?

Mark Kelly

1978. What is the name of Jerry Brown's father?
Pat Brown

1979. In which year did Bill Ritter marry Jeannie Ritter?
1983

1980. Can you name the politician who received the «Hoover Medal» in the year 1944?
Ralph Edward Flanders

1981. Can you name the politician who received the «Grammy Award for Best Spoken Word Album» in the year 1997?
Hillary Clinton

1982. Name any one award Mary Lou Makepeace received in the year 2008.
Colorado Women's Hall of Fame

1983. Can you name the politician who received the «Gallup's most admired man and woman poll» award in the year 2000?
Hillary Clinton

1984. Name any one award Franklin Delano Roosevelt received in the year 1932.
Time Person of the Year

1985. Name any one award Richard M. Daley received in the year 2007.
Newberry Library Award

1986. Name any one award George H. W. Bush received in the year 1992.
Doublespeak Award

1987. Can you name the politician who received the «Honorary citizen of Kraków» award in the year 1996?
Hank Brown

1988. Can you name the politician who received the «ASCB Public Service Award» in the year 2005?
Arlen Specter

1989. Russ Feingold, who belonged to the Democratic Party, became a senator in the year 1997. Which state did he represent?
Wisconsin

1990. Where was Susan Collins, a Republican senator from Maine, born?
Caribou

1991. In the year 1987, Xavier Becerra worked as Deputy Attorney General in which justice ministry?
California Department of Justice

1992. Whom did Jesse Jackson Jr. marry in the year 1991?
Sandi Jackson

1993. From which university did Noreen Evans get her bachelor's degree in government?
California State University, Sacramento

1994. From which university did Doug Jones get his Bachelor of Science degree in political science?
University of Alabama

1995. Can you name the politician who received the «Albert Lasker Award for Basic Medical Research» in the year 1954?

Albert Szent-Györgyi

1996. Richard Bryan, who belonged to the Democratic Party, became a senator in the year 1997. Which state did he represent?
Nevada

1997. John McCain became a US senator from Arizona in the year 1987. Where was he born?
Coco Solo

1998. Richard Shelby became a US senator from Alabama in the year 1993. Where was he born?
Birmingham

1999. Name any one award Earl Warren received in the year 1969.
honorary doctor of the Hebrew University of Jerusalem

2000. What is the name of Lincoln Chafee's father?
John Chafee

2001. Where was Bill Bradley, a Democratic senator from New Jersey, born?
Crystal City

2002. Jon Kyl, who belonged to the Republican Party, became a senator in the year 2018. Which state did he represent?
Arizona

2003. What medal did Yehudi Menuhin receive in the year 1962?
Royal Philharmonic Society Gold Medal

2004. What is the name of Michael Bloomberg's father?
William Henry Bloomberg

2005. Who replaced Pete Wilson as the senator from California in the year 1983?
John Seymour

2006. In which year did Bruce Babbitt become the Governor of Arizona?
1978

2007. Can you name the politician who received the «Distinguished Americans series» award in the year 2000?
Claude Denson Pepper

2008. Can you name the politician who received the «Gandhi Peace Award» in the year 1960?
Eleanor Roosevelt

2009. Olympia Snowe became a senator in the year 2005. Which state did she represent?
Maine

2010. Can you name the politician who received the «National Women's Hall of Fame» award in the year 1998?
Madeleine Albright

2011. In which year did Gerald L. Baliles become the Governor of Virginia?
1986

2012. Can you name the politician who received the «Labor Hall of Honor» award in the year 1990?
Robert Ferdinand Wagner

2013. Can you name the politician who received the «J. Walter Kennedy Citizenship Award» in the year 1991?
Kevin Johnson

2014. Name any one award Richard Lugar received in the year 2012.
Knight of Freedom Award

2015. Chuck Grassley, who belonged to the Republican Party, became a senator in the year 2007. Which state did he represent?
Iowa

2016. Can you name the politician who received the «Theodore Roosevelt Award» in the year 1990?
Ronald Reagan

2017. Orrin Hatch became a senator in the year 1993. Which state did he represent?
Utah

2018. Whom did Clarence Thomas marry in the year 1987?
Virginia Lamp Thomas

2019. What is the name of Ben Quayle's mother?
Marilyn Quayle

2020. From which university did Dale Denno get his Bachelor of Arts degree in political science?
Syracuse University

2021. Donald W. Riegle, Jr. became a US senator from Michigan in the year 1976. Where was he born?
Flint

2022. Can you name the politician who received the «Lasker-Bloomberg Public Service Award» in the year 1963?
Melvin Laird

2023. Who became the mayor of Indianapolis in the year 1968?
Richard Lugar

2024. Pete Domenici became a US senator from New Mexico in the year 1999. Where was he born?
Albuquerque

2025. In which year did Paul Ryan marry Janna Little?
2000

2026. Can you name the politician who received the «collar of the Order of the Aztec Eagle» award in the year 2018?
Jared Kushner

2027. Can you name the politician who received the «Spingarn Medal» in the year 1987?
Percy Sutton

2028. Tom Harkin became a senator in the year 1997. Which state did he represent?
Iowa

2029. What medal did Coleman Young get in the year 1981?
Spingarn Medal

2030. Patrick Joseph Toomey became a senator in the year 2015. Which state did he represent?
Pennsylvania

2031. Can you name the politician who received the «Arthur L. Schawlow Prize in Laser Science» in the year 1994?
Steven Chu

2032. Where was Jim Jeffords, a Republican senator from Vermont, born?
Rutland

2033. Where did Mike Pence get his bachelor's degree in study of history from?
Hanover College

2034. Who replaced Ted Kaufman as the senator from Delaware in the year 2009?
Chris Coons

2035. Jay Rockefeller, who belonged to the Democratic Party, became a senator in the year 1991. Which state did he represent?
West Virginia

2036. Hank Brown became a senator in the year 1991. Which state did he represent?
Colorado

2037. In which year did Geraldine Ferraro marry John Zaccaro?
1960

2038. Bob Kerrey became a senator in the year 1989. Which state did he represent?
Nebraska

2039. In which year did Charlie Crist marry Carole Crist?
2008

2040. Can you name the politician who received the «Indira Gandhi Prize» in the year 1997?
Jimmy Carter

2041. What is the name of Jared Polis's father?

Stephen Schutz

2042. In the year 2003, whom did John Baldacci succeed as the Governor of Maine?
Angus King

2043. Name any one award Geraldine Ferraro received in the year 1994.
National Women's Hall of Fame

2044. Name any one award Al Gore received in the year 2009.
Roger Revelle Prize

2045. Name any one award Lawrence Summers received in the year 2007.
honorary doctor of Harvard University

2046. In which year did Gavin Newsom marry Kimberly Guilfoyle?
2001

2047. Name any one award George F. Kennan received in the year 1957.
Pulitzer Prize for History

2048. Can you name the politician who received the «Theodore Roosevelt Award» in the year 2009?
Madeleine Albright

2049. Who wrote the book «Nomad: From Islam to America»?
Ayaan Hirsi Ali

2050. Who succeeded Matt Claman as the mayor of Anchorage in the year 2009?
Dan Sullivan

2051. In the year 1974, Brad Ashford worked as a lawyer in which government agency?
Federal Highway Administration

2052. Robert Jones Portman became a senator in the year 2011. Which state did he represent?
Ohio

2053. John Breaux, who belonged to the Democratic Party, became a senator in the year 1999. Which state did he represent?
Louisiana

2054. Where was Thad Cochran, a Republican senator from Mississippi, born?
Pontotoc

2055. Name any one award George P. Shultz received in the year 1992.
Sylvanus Thayer Award

2056. Who became the mayor of Yankton in the year 1995?
Jean Hunhoff

2057. Can you name the politician who received the «Sierra Club John Muir Award» in the year 2007?
Al Gore

2058. Where did Jacob Frey get his bachelor's degree in government from?
College of William & Mary

2059. Name any one award Dick Armey received in the year 2010.
Doublespeak Award

2060. Can you name the politician who received the «Doublespeak Award» in the year 2015?
Joni Ernst

2061. From which college did Patricia Harris get her Bachelor of Arts degree in government?
Franklin & Marshall College

2062. Max Baucus became a US senator from Montana in the year 1978. Where was he born?
Helena

2063. Where did Barack Obama get his Bachelor of Arts degree in political science from?
Columbia University

2064. John McCain, who belonged to the Republican Party, became a senator in the year 2013. Which state did he represent?
Arizona

2065. Name any one award Hiram Johnson received in the year 2009.
California Hall of Fame

2066. Can you name the politician who received the «Time 100» award in the year 2014?
Hillary Clinton

2067. Whom did Jane Byrne marry in the year 1978?
Jay McMullen

2068. What is the name of Bernie Sanders's father?
Eli Sanders

2069. Ted Kennedy became a US senator from

Massachusetts in the year 2001. Where was he born?
Boston

2070. In the year 2003, whom did Jim Douglas succeed as the Governor of Vermont?
Howard Dean

2071. Whom did Meg Whitman marry in the year 1980?
Griffith R. Harsh

2072. Where was Michael Bennet, a Democratic senator from Colorado, born?
New Delhi

2073. Where was John Boozman, a Republican senator from Arkansas, born?
Shreveport

2074. John Hoeven, who belonged to the Republican Party, became a senator in the year 2015. Which state did he represent?
North Dakota

2075. Name any one award Alan Greenspan received in the year 1996.
Francis Boyer Award

2076. In which year did Bob Ehrlich become the Governor of Maryland?
2003

2077. Sam Brownback became a senator in the year 1999. Which state did he represent?
Kansas

2078. Can you name the politician who received the «Otto Hahn Peace Medal» in the year 2018?

John Kerry

2079. Charles Ellis Schumer became a US senator from New York in the year 2011. Where was he born?
Brooklyn

2080. Connie Mack III became a senator in the year 1993. Which state did he represent?
Florida

2081. Can you name the politician who received the «Spingarn Medal» in the year 1985?
Tom Bradley

2082. What medal did John J. McCloy receive in the year 1975?
Ernst Reuter Medal

2083. Where did George W. Bush get his Bachelor of Arts degree in history from?
Yale College

2084. Can you name the politician who received the «Freedom Award» in the year 1959?
William J. Donovan

2085. Where was Jeff Flake, a Republican senator from Arizona, born?
Snowflake

2086. Can you name the politician who received the «Michigan Women's Hall of Fame» award in the year 2016?
Daisy Elliott

2087. Where was Mary Kathryn Heitkamp, a senator from North Dakota, born?

Breckenridge

2088. John Ensign became a US senator from Nevada in the year 2003. Where was he born?
Roseville

2089. In which year did Gavin Newsom marry Jennifer Siebel?
2008

2090. Whom did Chris Christie marry in the year 1986?
Mary Pat Christie

2091. Who had hired Peter Roskam as a member of congressional staff in the year 1986?
Henry Hyde

2092. Name any one award Kathy Osterman received in the year 1993.
Chicago Gay and Lesbian Hall of Fame

2093. Can you name the politician who received the «Honorary citizen of Kraków» award in the year 1994?
George H. W. Bush

2094. Can you name the politician who received the «John Simon Guggenheim Memorial Foundation Fellowship» award in the year 1996?
Steven Chu

2095. What medal did Vannevar Bush get in the year 1949?
IRI Medal

2096. In the year 1969, Byron Dorgan worked as a delegate in which political party?
North Dakota Democratic Party

2097. In the year 1975, whom did David L. Boren succeed as the Governor of Oklahoma?
David Hall

2098. Maria Cantwell, who belonged to the Democratic Party, became a senator in the year 2015. Which state did she represent?
Washington

2099. Can you name the politician who received the «Honorary doctor of the Humboldt University of Berlin» award in the year 2010?
Joseph H. H. Weiler

2100. In the year 2003, whom did Bill Richardson succeed as the Governor of New Mexico?
Gary Johnson

2101. Who had hired John Neely Kennedy as a secretary of state in the year 1996?
Murphy J. Foster

2102. Where did Nancy Pelosi get her Bachelor of Arts degree in political science from?
Trinity Washington University

2103. Can you name the politician who received the «Order of the Cross of Terra Mariana, 1st Class» award in the year 2002?
John McCain

2104. Can you name the politician who received the «Eleanor Roosevelt Award for Human Rights» in the year 2001?
Frank Wolf

2105. In which year did Corine Mauch marry Juliana Müller?
2014

2106. Name any one award Jocelyn Benson received in the year 2015.
Michigan Women's Hall of Fame

2107. Name any one award Edward L. Ayers received in the year 2004.
Bancroft Prize

2108. Olympia Snowe became a senator in the year 2011. Which state did she represent?
Maine

2109. Norm Coleman, who belonged to the Republican Party, became a senator in the year 2005. Which state did he represent?
Minnesota

2110. Name any one award Richard Lugar received in the year 2002.
Order of the Cross of Terra Mariana, 1st Class

2111. Mark Takano worked as a member of which community college district in the year 1990?
Riverside Community College District

2112. In the year 2011, whom did Robert J. Bentley succeed as the Governor of Alabama?
Bob Riley

2113. Whom did Mike Pence marry in the year 1985?
Karen Pence

2114. Richard Lugar became a US senator from Indiana in

the year 1999. Where was he born?
Indianapolis

2115. Pete Domenici became a senator in the year 1997. Which state did he represent?
New Mexico

2116. From which university did Kevin Johnson get his bachelor's degree in political science?
University of California, Berkeley

2117. Where was Joe Lieberman, a senator from Connecticut, born?
Stamford

2118. In the year 1988, Bob Franks worked as a chairperson in which political party?
New Jersey Republican State Committee

2119. Can you name the politician who received the «James Madison Award» in the year 1999?
Henry Waxman

2120. In which year did Bobby Jindal become the Governor of Louisiana?
2008

2121. Who wrote the book «Citizenville: How to Take the Town Square Digital and Reinvent Government»?
Gavin Newsom

2122. Name any one award Colin Powell received in the year 1991.
Horatio Alger Award

2123. What is the name of Patrick J. Kennedy's mother?
Joan Bennett Kennedy

2124. Orrin Hatch became a US senator from Utah in the year 2017. Where was he born?
Homestead Park

2125. Whom did Boris Johnson marry in the year 1993?
Marina Wheeler

2126. From which university did Patrick H. Lyons get his Bachelor of Science degree in agricultural economics?
New Mexico State University

2127. From which university did Jim Risch get his Bachelor of Science degree in forestry?
University of Idaho

2128. Whom did Sonny Bono marry in the year 1986?
Mary Bono

2129. Where was Harry Reid, a Democratic senator from Nevada, born?
Searchlight

2130. In the year 1987, whom did George S. Mickelson succeed as the Governor of South Dakota?
Bill Janklow

2131. Ben Nighthorse Campbell became a senator in the year 2003. Which state did he represent?
Colorado

2132. Can you name the politician who received the «Holley Medal» in the year 1943?
Vannevar Bush

2133. Bob Krueger became a US senator from Texas in the year 1993. Where was he born?

New Braunfels

2134. Whom did Richard Holbrooke marry in the year 1995?
Kati Marton

2135. In which year did Douglas Wilder become the Governor of Virginia?
1990

2136. In which year did Lamar Alexander become the Governor of Tennessee?
1979

2137. In the year 1999, whom did Jeb Bush succeed as the Governor of Florida?
Buddy MacKay

2138. Name any one award Joe Lieberman received in the year 2012.
Ewald von Kleist award

2139. Can you name the politician who received the «Jubilee Medal "In Commemoration of the 100th Anniversary of the Birth of Vladimir Ilyich Lenin"» in the year 1972?
Angela Davis

2140. In which year did Ted Kennedy marry Victoria Reggie Kennedy?
1992

2141. Ted Kennedy became a senator in the year 2005. Which state did he represent?
Massachusetts

2142. Dirk Kempthorne became a senator in the year 1995.

Which state did he represent?
Idaho

2143. In which year did Howard Dean become the Governor of Vermont?
1991

2144. Can you name the politician who received the «Dan David Prize» in the year 2008?
Al Gore

2145. Where was Dennis DeConcini, a senator from Arizona, born?
Tucson

2146. Where did George Voinovich get his Bachelor of Arts degree in government from?
Ohio University

2147. In the year 2009, whom did Sean Parnell succeed as the Governor of Alaska?
Sarah Palin

2148. Where did Denise Driehaus get her bachelor's degree in political science from?
Miami University

2149. Who became the mayor of Tallahassee in the year 2014?
Andrew Gillum

2150. Name any one award Henry Kissinger received in the year 1976.
Knight Grand Cross of the Order of Merit of the Italian Republic

2151. In the year 1979, whom did Robert List succeed as

the Governor of Nevada?
Mike O'Callaghan

2152. What medal did Hillary Clinton get in the year 2009?
Four Freedoms Award - Freedom Medal

2153. Who had hired Dick Durbin as a legal counsel in the year 1969?
Paul Simon

2154. Jim Bunning became a senator in the year 1999. Which state did he represent?
Kentucky

2155. What medal did J. Lister Hill get in the year 1969?
Public Welfare Medal

2156. Can you name the politician who received the «Hoover Medal» in the year 1967?
Lucius D. Clay

2157. Where did Ryan Zinke get his Master of Business Administration degree in finance from?
National University

2158. Barbara Boxer became a US senator from California in the year 1995. Where was she born?
Brooklyn

2159. Craig L. Thomas became a senator in the year 2007. Which state did he represent?
Wyoming

2160. Who had hired Peter Roskam as a member of congressional staff in the year 1985?
Tom DeLay

2161. From which university did Patrick H. Lyons get his Master of Science degree in agricultural science?
Colorado State University

2162. Name any one award Al Gore received in the year 2012.
Internet Hall of Fame

2163. Where did Karen Heck get her bachelor's degree in government from?
Colby College

2164. Name any one award Barbara Jordan received in the year 1993.
Elizabeth Blackwell Award

2165. Who replaced David L. Boren as the senator from Oklahoma in the year 1979?
Jim Mountain Inhofe

2166. Whom did Pete Domenici replace as the senator from New Mexico in the year 1973?
Clinton Presba Anderson

2167. In the year 2001, whom did Scott McCallum succeed as the Governor of Wisconsin?
Tommy Thompson

2168. Name any one award Barney Frank received in the year 2014.
Humanist of the Year

2169. Whom did Paul Wellstone marry in the year 1963?
Sheila Wellstone

2170. Name any one award Jimmy Carter received in the year 2012.

Honorary doctor at the Nanjing University

2171. Rand Paul became a US senator from Kentucky in the year 2015. Where was he born?
Pittsburgh

2172. Ben Nelson, who belonged to the Democratic Party, became a senator in the year 2007. Which state did he represent?
Nebraska

2173. In the year 1974, whom did Julian Carroll succeed as the Governor of Kentucky?
Wendell H. Ford

2174. George LeMieux became a US senator from Florida in the year 2009. Where was he born?
Fort Lauderdale

2175. Name any one award Russell W. Peterson received in the year 1978.
William Procter Prize for Scientific Achievement

2176. What is the name of Boris Johnson's mother?
Charlotte Johnson Wahl

2177. Where was Trent Lott, a Republican senator from Mississippi, born?
Grenada

2178. Can you name the politician who received the «Sierra Club John Muir Award» in the year 2002?
Jim Jeffords

2179. Can you name the politician who received the «Eleanor Roosevelt Award for Human Rights» in the year 1998?

John Lewis

2180. Phil Gramm became a senator in the year 1985. Which state did he represent?
Texas

2181. Can you name the politician who received the «Light of Truth Award» in the year 2003?
Benjamin A. Gilman

2182. In which year did Neil Goldschmidt become the Governor of Oregon?
1987

2183. What is the name of William M. Daley's mother?
Eleanor "Sis" Daley

2184. Ben Sasse became a US senator from Nebraska in the year 2015. Where was he born?
Plainview

2185. Cindy Hyde-Smith became a US senator from Mississippi in the year 2018. Where was she born?
Brookhaven

2186. Can you name the politician who received the «Sagamore of the Wabash» award in the year 1996?
John R. Gregg

2187. Can you name the politician who received the «Candace Award» in the year 1992?
Maxine Waters

2188. Can you name the politician who received the «Chicago Gay and Lesbian Hall of Fame» award in the year 2012?
David Duvall Orr

2189. Whom did Kit Bond replace as the senator from Missouri in the year 1987?
Thomas Eagleton

2190. Whom did Rudy Giuliani marry in the year 2003?
Judith Giuliani

2191. Can you name the politician who received the «J. Walter Kennedy Citizenship Award» in the year 1996?
Chris Dudley

2192. Where was Al Franken, a Democratic senator from Minnesota, born?
Manhattan

2193. From which university did Meg Whitman get her Bachelor of Science degree in economics?
Princeton University

2194. In the year 2003, whom did Jim Doyle succeed as the Governor of Wisconsin?
Scott McCallum

2195. Dean Heller became a senator in the year 2017. Which state did he represent?
Nevada

2196. Sherrod Brown became a senator in the year 2007. Which state did he represent?
Ohio

2197. What is the name of Jay Rockefeller's father?
John D. Rockefeller III

2198. Luther Strange became a US senator from Alabama in the year 2017. Where was he born?

Birmingham

2199. What is the name of Lawrence Summers's father?
Robert Summers

2200. Name any one award Claude Denson Pepper received in the year 1967.
Lasker-Bloomberg Public Service Award

2201. What is the name of Donald Trump's mother?
Mary Anne MacLeod

2202. In the year 1985, Lamar Alexander worked as a chairperson in which organization?
National Governors Association

2203. In which year did Mike Pence become the Governor of Indiana?
2013

2204. Name any one award Annie Dodge Wauneka received in the year 2000.
National Women's Hall of Fame

2205. Can you name the politician who received the «Pulitzer Prize for Biography or Autobiography» in the year 1968?
George F. Kennan

2206. Chuck Grassley, who belonged to the Republican Party, became a senator in the year 1999. Which state did he represent?
Iowa

2207. In the year 1995, whom did Angus King succeed as the Governor of Maine?
John R. McKernan

2208. Where did Boris Johnson get his Bachelor of Arts degree in classics from?
Balliol College

2209. Can you name the politician who received the «honorary doctor of Harvard University» award in the year 2013?
Thomas Menino

2210. Can you name the politician who received the «Colorado Women's Hall of Fame» award in the year 2014?
Helen Ring Robinson

2211. In which year did Tim Kaine marry Anne Holton?
1984

2212. What medal did Robert McNamara receive in the year 1968?
Presidential Medal of Freedom

2213. Rand Paul became a senator in the year 2017. Which state did he represent?
Kentucky

2214. Can you name the politician who received the «WWE Hall of Fame» award in the year 2013?
Donald Trump

2215. In the year 1985, whom did Norman H. Bangerter succeed as the Governor of Utah?
Scott M. Matheson

2216. In the year 1994, whom did Froilan Tenorio succeed as the Governor of the Northern Mariana Islands?
Lorenzo I. De Leon Guerrero

2217. Where did Hillary Clinton work as a board member in the year 1990?
Lafarge

2218. Can you name the politician who received the «NAACP Image Award for Outstanding Literary Work, Nonfiction» in the year 2007?
Barack Obama

2219. Name any one award George McGovern received in the year 1991.
Gandhi Peace Award

2220. Who replaced Jeff Flake as the senator from Arizona in the year 2013?
Kyrsten Sinema

2221. What medal did Jimmy Carter receive in the year 1998?
Hoover Medal

2222. From which university did Ryan Zinke get his Bachelor of Science degree in geology?
University of Oregon

2223. Where was Claire McCaskill, a senator from Missouri, born?
Rolla

2224. Can you name the politician who received the «Musikpreis der Stadt Duisburg» award in the year 1992?
Yehudi Menuhin

2225. In the year 1997, whom did Gary Locke succeed as the Governor of Washington?
Mike Lowry

2226. What medal did Thurgood Marshall receive in the year 1946?
Spingarn Medal

2227. Can you name the politician who received the «Grammy Award for Best Spoken Word Album» in the year 2006?
Barack Obama

2228. Who became the mayor of Little Rock in the year 2007?
Mark Stodola

2229. Name any one award Vannevar Bush received in the year 1946.
Washington Award

2230. In which year did Forrest Hood James, Jr. become the Governor of Alabama?
1995

2231. Can you name the politician who received the «Theodore Roosevelt Award» in the year 2004?
Alan Page

2232. Where was Angus King, a senator from Maine, born?
Alexandria

2233. Where was John Thune, a Republican senator from South Dakota, born?
Pierre

2234. Name any one award Dave Bing received in the year 1968.
All-NBA Team

2235. In which year did Michael Huffington marry Arianna Huffington?
1985

2236. Where was Bob Kerrey, a Democratic senator from Nebraska, born?
Lincoln

2237. Can you name the politician who received the «National Women's Hall of Fame» award in the year 1993?
Jeannette Rankin

2238. Where was Larry Craig, a Republican senator from Idaho, born?
Council

2239. Name any one award Patricia Roberts Harris received in the year 2003.
National Women's Hall of Fame

2240. Name any one award Richard Lamm received in the year 1993.
Humanist of the Year

2241. Name any one award Mumia Abu-Jamal received in the year 2001.
Honorary citizen of Paris

2242. What medal did Henry Ford receive in the year 1936?
Holley Medal

2243. Bob P. Casey, Jr. became a US senator from Pennsylvania in the year 2011. Where was he born?
Scranton

2244. Ron Lee Wyden, who belonged to the Democratic Party, became a senator in the year 2015. Which state did he represent?
Oregon

2245. Where did Ulysses Currie get his Master of Arts degree in pedagogy from?
American University

2246. Whom did Lois Capps marry in the year 1960?
Walter Capps

2247. Where did Alexander Acosta work as a dean in the year 2009?
Florida International University College of Law

2248. In the year 2015, Kevin Elsenheimer worked as a director in which government agency?
Michigan State Housing Development Authority

2249. In which year did Susana Martinez marry Chuck Franco?
1991

2250. Who became the mayor of Madison in the year 1989?
Paul Soglin

2251. Name any one award John Lewis received in the year 1998.
Lillian Smith Book Award

2252. Can you name the politician who received the «James Madison Award» in the year 1993?
Ted Stevens

2253. Mike DeWine became a US senator from Ohio in the

year 1995. Where was he born?
Springfield

2254. Can you name the politician who received the «Wilbur Cross Medal» in the year 2006?
Richard Brodhead I

2255. Whom did Carte Goodwin replace as the senator from West Virginia in the year 2010?
Robert Byrd

2256. In the year 2010, Daniel S. Sullivan worked as Government Commissioner in which state agency of the United States?
Alaska Department of Natural Resources

2257. John McCain, who belonged to the Republican Party, became a senator in the year 1999. Which state did he represent?
Arizona

2258. Name any one award Oveta Culp Hobby received in the year 2011.
Distinguished Americans series

2259. Name any one award Herman Cain received in the year 1996.
Horatio Alger Award

2260. In the year 1983, whom did Bob Kerrey succeed as the Governor of Nebraska?
Charles Thone

2261. Ted Kennedy became a US senator from Massachusetts in the year 2003. Where was he born?
Boston

2262. Evan Bayh became a US senator from Indiana in the year 1999. Where was he born?
Shirkieville

2263. In the year 1993, whom did James Elisha Folsom, Jr. succeed as the Governor of Alabama?
Harold Guy Hunt

2264. Jim Risch became a senator in the year 2017. Which state did he represent?
Idaho

2265. Where was Lindsey Graham, a Republican senator from South Carolina, born?
Central

2266. In which year did Arianna Huffington marry Michael Huffington?
1985

2267. Can you name the politician who received the «Academy Honorary Award» in the year 2016?
Jackie Chan

2268. Name any one award Cyrus Vance received in the year 1992.
Freedom Award

2269. Name any one award Jay Rockefeller received in the year 2013.
Order of the Rising Sun, 1st class

2270. George Voinovich, who belonged to the Republican Party, became a senator in the year 2003. Which state did he represent?
Ohio

2271. Name any one award Condoleezza Rice received in the year 2007.
Eric-M.-Warburg-Award

2272. Can you name the politician who received the «Gaming Hall of Fame» award in the year 1995?
Donald Trump

2273. Name any one award Yehudi Menuhin received in the year 1972.
Léonie Sonning Music Prize

2274. Can you name the politician who received the «Siena Medal» in the year 1947?
Mary Teresa Norton

2275. Jay Rockefeller, who belonged to the Democratic Party, became a senator in the year 2001. Which state did he represent?
West Virginia

2276. What is the name of William M. Daley's father?
Richard J. Daley

2277. In the year 2011, whom did Terry Branstad succeed as the Governor of Iowa?
Chet Culver

2278. Patrick Leahy became a US senator from Vermont in the year 2003. Where was he born?
Montpelier

2279. Where did Bob Bennett work as a chief executive officer in the year 1984?
FranklinCovey

2280. Whom did Ken Salazar replace as the senator from

Colorado in the year 2005?
Ben Nighthorse Campbell

2281. Mike DeWine, who belonged to the Republican Party, became a senator in the year 1997. Which state did he represent?
Ohio

2282. In which year did Phil Bredesen become the Governor of Tennessee?
2003

2283. Brian Schatz became a US senator from Hawaii in the year 2013. Where was he born?
Ann Arbor

2284. Can you name the politician who received the «Freedom Award» in the year 2012?
John C. Whitehead

2285. In which year did Bob Miller become the Governor of Nevada?
1989

2286. Where was Robert C. Smith, a Republican senator from New Hampshire, born?
Trenton

2287. Whom did Newt Gingrich marry in the year 1981?
Marianne Ginther

2288. Barbara Boxer became a US senator from California in the year 2011. Where was she born?
Brooklyn

2289. Where was John Ensign, a Republican senator from Nevada, born?

Roseville

2290. Robert Menendez became a US senator from New Jersey in the year 2006. Where was he born?
Uranus

2291. Tim Johnson became a senator in the year 2009. Which state did he represent?
South Dakota

2292. Jim DeMint became a US senator from South Carolina in the year 2009. Where was he born?
Greenville

2293. What is the name of John Kerry's father?
Richard J. Kerry

2294. Can you name the politician who received the «James Madison Award» in the year 1994?
Hazel R. O'Leary

2295. Name any one award Alexander Haig received in the year 1981.
Doublespeak Award

2296. Name any one award Ella T. Grasso received in the year 1993.
National Women's Hall of Fame

2297. Bob Graham became a senator in the year 1987. Which state did he represent?
Florida

2298. Can you name the politician who received the «EFF Pioneer Award» in the year 2001?
Bruce Ennis

2299. Who had hired Darin LaHood as a member of congressional staff in the year 1990?
Jerry Lewis

2300. What is the name of Michael Bennet's father?
Douglas J. Bennet

2301. Ciro Rodriguez worked as a member of which school district in the year 1975?
Harlandale Independent School District

2302. Name any one award Walter Mondale received in the year 1996.
Person of the Year, American Chamber of Commerce in Japan

2303. Where did Sarah Palin get her bachelor's degree in journalism from?
University of Idaho

2304. Jeff Bingaman became a US senator from New Mexico in the year 1983. Where was he born?
El Paso

THE END

Thanks for reading!
Copyright © 2019 Meghan A. Faith